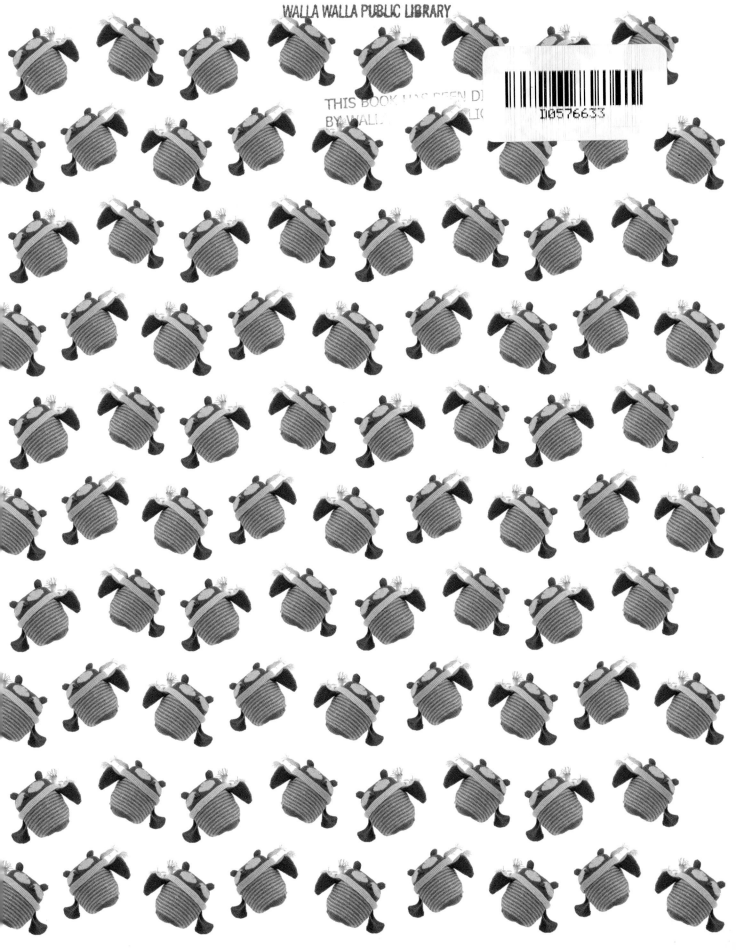

LUCINDA GUY

AND SO TO BED...

LUCINDA GUY

AND SO TO BED...

24 ORIGINAL HANDKNITS FOR GIRLS AND BOYS

Illustrations by François Hall

Trafalgar Square Publishing

North Pomfret, Vermont

This book is dedicated to Maurice

First published in the United States of America in 2006
by Trafalgar Square Publishing
North Pomfret, Vermont 05053

Printed in Singapore

Designs by Lucinda Guy
Photography, illustrations, and layout by François Hall
Editor Sally Harding
Pattern writer Sue Whiting
Pattern checkers Stella Smith and Marilyn Wilson

Library of Congress Control Number: 2005910795

ISBN-13: 978-1-57076-329-8
ISBN-10: 1-57076-329-1

CONTENTS

INTRODUCTION

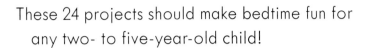

These 24 projects should make bedtime fun for any two- to five-year-old child!

There is a sweet cotton bunny as well as a doll to knit, each with its very own special outfit. Bella Bunny has a lovely top and full skirt that ties with a little silk ribbon, and Lula Doll has a pretty flowery dress, dainty slippers, and matching underwear. There is also a naughty, up-to-no-good fox and a contemplative owl who both wear woolly scarves.

All the projects should please the average knitter, from simple classic bathrobes, cardigans, and tank tops, to more elaborate knits such as the embroidered Roost Blanket and the Moon Hot Water Bottle Cover. There are simple stripy socks, slippers, pajama cases, and even a cute nightcap to complement the outfits and blankets.

All the garments are knitted in Rowan's beautiful Cashsoft DK and Cashsoft Baby DK, which are wonderfully soft, warm, and comforting. The sumptuous muted colors all add to the charm of the collection. These yarns are machine washable, so the garments are not only sweet and charming but practical, too!

This collection will be a pleasure to knit and should be enjoyed and treasured for many years to come.

SLEEPYHEAD BATHROBE

This pretty little bathrobe with its sweet, sleepy-face pockets will keep you warm and cozy as you get ready for bed.

BEFORE YOU BEGIN

YARN

Sizes	2-3 yrs	3-4 yrs	4-5 yrs
To fit chest	22in	24in	26in
	56cm	61cm	66cm
Actual size	26½in	28¾in	30¾in
	67cm	73cm	78cm
Back length	19in	21in	22½in
	48cm	53cm	57cm
Underarm seam, with	8½in	10¼in	12in
cuff folded back	22cm	26cm	30cm

Rowan RYC Cashsoft Baby DK and Cashsoft DK			
A Baby DK Pale blue (805)	6	7	8 x 50g/1¾oz
B Baby DK Lemon (802)	1	1	1 x 50g/1¾oz
C Baby DK Pink (807)	1	1	1 x 50g/1¾oz
D DK Deep pink (506)	1	1	1 x 50g/1¾oz

NEEDLES & HOOK
1 pair each of size 5 (3.75mm) and size 6 (4mm) needles.
Size E/4 (3.50mm) crochet hook.

BUTTONS
4

GAUGE
22 sts and 30 rows = 4in [10cm] square measured over St st using size 6 (4mm) needles.

GETTING STARTED

BACK
Using size 5 (3.75mm) needles and yarn A, cast on 92 (100: 108) sts.
Work in g st for 10 rows, ending with RS facing for next row.
Change to size 6 (4mm) needles.
Beg with a K row, work in St st, shaping side seams by dec 1 st at each end of 7th and every foll 8th row until 74 (80: 86) sts rem.
Work even until back meas 13 (14½: 15¾)in

[33 (37: 40)cm], ending with RS facing for next row.
Change to size 5 (3.75mm) needles.
Work in g st for 14 rows, ending with RS facing for next row.

Shape armholes
Dec 1 st at each end of next 4 rows. 66 (72: 78) sts.
Work even until armhole meas 4¼ (4¾: 5)in [11 (12: 13)cm], ending with RS facing for next row.

Shape back neck
Next row (RS) K24 (26: 28) and turn, leaving rem sts on a holder.
Work each side of neck separately.
Bind off 4 sts at beg of next row, then 3 sts at beg of foll alt row, ending with RS facing for next row. 17 (19: 21) sts.

Shape shoulder
Bind off.
With RS facing, rejoin yarn to rem sts, bind off center 18 (20: 22) sts, K to end. 24 (26: 28) sts.
Complete to match first side, reversing shapings.

LEFT FRONT
Using size 5 (3.75mm) needles and yarn A, cast on 46 (50: 54) sts.
Work in g st for 10 rows, ending with RS facing for next row.
Change to size 6 (4mm) needles.
Beg with a K row, work in St st, shaping side seam by dec 1 st at beg of 7th and every foll 8th row until 37 (40: 43) sts rem.
Work even until left front meas 13 (14½: 15¾)in [33 37: 40)cm], ending with RS facing for next row.
Change to size 5 (3.75mm) needles.
Next row (RS) K to end, turn and cast on 12 sts. 49 (52: 55) sts.

Work in g st for 8 rows, ending with **WS** facing for next row.
Bind off 12 sts at beg of next row. 37 (40: 43) sts.
Work 4 rows, ending with RS facing for next row.

Shape armhole

Dec 1 st at beg of next row, then at same edge on foll 3 rows. 33 (36: 39) sts.
Work even until left front matches back to shoulder bind-off, ending with RS facing for next row.

Shape shoulder and collar turn-back

Bind off all sts, placing marker after 17th (19th: 21st) st from armhole edge to mark neck shoulder point.

RIGHT FRONT

Using size 5 (3.75mm) needles and yarn A, cast on 46 (50: 54) sts.
Work in g st for 10 rows, ending with RS facing for next row.
Change to size 6 (4mm) needles.
Beg with a K row, work in St st, shaping side seam by dec 1 st at end of 7th and every foll 8th row until 37 (40: 43) sts rem.
Work even until right front meas 13 (14½: 15¾) in [33 (37: 40) cm], ending with RS facing for next row.

Change to size 5 (3.75mm) needles.
Next row (RS) Cast on 12 sts, K to end. 49 (52: 55) sts.
Work in g st for 3 rows, ending with RS facing for next row.
Next row (RS) *K3, K2tog, yo (to make a buttonhole), rep from * 3 times more, K to end.
Work in g st for 5 rows, ending with RS facing for next row.
Bind off 12 sts at beg of next row. 37 (40: 43) sts.
Complete to match left front, reversing shapings.

SLEEVES

Using size 5 (3.75mm) needles and yarn A, cast on 34 (36: 38) sts.

Work in g st, shaping sides by inc 1 st at each end of 21st and every foll 6th (6th: 8th) row until there are 46 (40: 56) sts, then on every foll 8th (8th: 10th) row until there are 54 (58: 62) sts. Work even until sleeve meas 9¾ (11½: 13) in [25 (29: 33) cm], ending with RS facing for next row.

Shape sleeve cap
Dec 1 st at each end of next 4 rows.
Bind off rem 46 (50: 54) sts.

POCKETS (make 2)
Using size 6 (4mm) needles and yarn A, cast on 15 sts.

Using the *intarsia* technique, work foll face chart, which is worked entirely in St st beg with a K row, as follows:

Chart row 1 (RS) Using A, knit.
Keeping chart patt correct, inc 1 st at each end of next 2 rows. 19 sts.
Rep last 3 rows once more, then first 2 of these rows again. 25 sts.
Work even until all 18 rows of chart have been completed, ending with RS facing for next row.
Break off contrasts and cont in St st using yarn A only.
Work 5 rows, dec 1 st at each end of 2nd of these rows and ending with **WS** facing for next row.
Next row (WS) Knit to form ridge.
Change to size 5 (3.75mm) needles.
Work 4 rows more in St st, beg with a K row.
Bind off.

FINISHING
Press pieces carefully on WS, using a warm iron over a damp cloth.
Sew both shoulder seams using backstitch, or mattress stitch if preferred.

Crochet edging
With RS facing, using size E/4 (3.50mm) crochet hook and yarn A, attach yarn at cast-on edge of right front opening edge and work 1 row of single crochet up entire shaped front opening edge, across collar turn-backs and back neck, then down entire shaped left front opening edge to left front cast-on edge. Fasten off.

Matching center of bound-off edge of sleeves to shoulder seams and shaped edges at underarm, sew sleeves into armholes. Sew side and sleeve seams, reversing sleeve seam for first 12 rows. Fold first 10 rows of sleeves to RS to form turn-back cuff and secure at sleeve seam. Using photograph as a guide, fold out collar turn-backs and secure in place.

Cheeks (make 4)
Using size 5 (3.75mm) needles and yarn D, cast on 11 sts.
Row 1 Knit.
Break off yarn, thread through all 11 sts, pull tight, and secure. Sew together ends of cast-on edge, so that strip forms a tiny disk.

Using chart as a guide, sew cheeks to pockets, and embroider eyelashes using yarn C. Fold last 4 rows of pockets to WS and slip stitch in place. Using six strands of yarn B, make two braids, each about 19½ in [50cm] long. Using photograph as a guide, form braid into looped curls and sew to top of pocket. Sew pockets to fronts. Sew on buttons.

KEY	
▨	A
	B
▥	C
⊡	place cheek
◺	long stitch

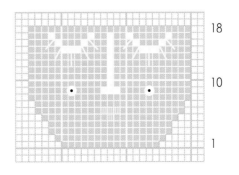

SLEEPYHEAD SLIPPERS

Don't forget that little toes also need to be kept warm and snug on their way to bed. These Sleepyhead Slippers are dreamy!

BEFORE YOU BEGIN

YARN

To fit	2-3 yrs	3-4 yrs	4-5 yrs
Length of foot	5½in	6½in	7in
	14.5cm	16cm	17.5cm

Rowan RYC Cashsoft Baby DK and Cashsoft DK			
A Baby DK Pale blue (805)	2	2	2 x 50g/1¾oz
B DK Deep pink (506)	1	1	1 x 50g/1¾oz
C Baby DK Pink (807)	small amount for all sizes		

NEEDLES & HOOK

1 pair each of size 2 (2.75mm) and size 3 (3mm) needles.
Size E/4 (3.50mm) crochet hook.

BUTTONS

2

GAUGE

25 sts and 46 rows = 4in [10cm] square measured over garter stitch using size 3 (3mm) needles.

GETTING STARTED

MAIN SECTION

Using size 3 (3mm) needles and yarn A, cast on 22 (24: 26) sts.
**Work in g st throughout as follows:
Work 1 row, ending with **WS** facing for next row.
Inc 1 st at each end of next and foll 6 (7: 8) alt rows. 36 (40: 44) sts.
Dec 1 st at each end of 2nd and foll 6 (7: 8) alt rows, ending with RS facing for next row. 22 (24: 26) sts.**
This section forms sole.

Shape upper

Cast on 7 (8: 9) sts (for heel) at beg of next row. 29 (32: 35) sts.
Inc 1 st at beg of next and foll 6 (7: 8) alt rows, ending with RS facing for next row. 36 (40: 44) sts.
Bind off 20 (22: 24) sts at beg of next row. 16 (18: 20) sts.
Work 13 (17: 21) rows, ending with RS facing for next row.
Cast on 20 (22: 24) sts at beg of next row. 36 (40: 44) sts.
This completes opening for foot.
Dec 1 st at beg of next and foll 6 (7: 8) alt rows, ending with RS facing for next row.
Bind off rem 29 (32: 35) sts.

INSOLE

Using size 2 (2.75mm) needles and yarn B, cast on 22 (24: 26) sts.
Work as given for main section from ** to **.
Bind off.

FINISHING

Do *not* press.

Sew heel seam, then sew upper to sole along shaped edges, easing in fullness of upper to fit sole.
Slip insole inside slipper and sew in place.

Strap

Using size 3 (3mm) needles and yarn A, starting and ending either side of heel seam, pick up and knit 18 (20: 22) sts across foot opening edge—9 (10: 11) sts at each side of heel seam.
Work in g st throughout as follows:
Cast on 14 (16: 18) sts at beg of next 2 rows. 46 (52: 58) sts.
Work 2 rows, ending with **WS** facing for next row.
Left slipper
Next row (WS) K to last 3 sts, yo, K2tog (to make a buttonhole), K1.
Right slipper
Next row (WS) K1, K2tog, yo (to make a buttonhole), K to end.

Both slippers

Work 2 rows more. Bind off.

Foot opening edging

With RS facing, using size E/4 (3.50mm) crochet hook and yarn A, attach yarn at base of strap and work 1 row of sc around foot opening to base of other edge of strap. Fasten off.

Flower

Using size E/4 (3.50mm) crochet hook and yarn B, ch3 and join with a slip st to form a ring.
Round 1 (RS) Ch1 (does *not* count as st), 8sc into ring, join with a slip st to first sc. Fasten off.
Make three more disks in this way.

Using photograph as a guide, position these four disks on top of foot and secure in place by working a French knot through all layers using yarn C.

Sew on button.

LULA DOLL & UNDERWEAR

Lula likes to look at books at bedtime. She especially likes books that have colorful pictures of flowers, animals, and stars in them.

YARN

Size of doll   12in [30cm] tall

Rowan 4-ply Cotton

A Beige (112)	1 x 50g/1¾oz
B Pink (120)	1 x 50g/1¾oz
C Mauve (130)	1 x 50g/1¾oz
D Pale green (131)	1 x 50g/1¾oz

Note: For the alternative underwear colorways, use B, C, and D where shown in photographs.

NEEDLES & HOOK

1 pair of size 2 (2.75mm) needles.
Size C/2 (2.50mm) crochet hook.

EXTRAS

Washable toy filling and 12in [30cm] of narrow ribbon.

GAUGE

29 sts and 38 rows = 4in [10cm] square measured over St st using size 2 (2.75mm) needles.

DOLL

BODY Ⓐ (make 2)

Using size 2 (2.75mm) needles and yarn A, cast on 26 sts.
Beg with a K row, work in St st as follows:
Work 1 row.
Inc 1 st at each end of next 2 rows. 30 sts.
Work 5 rows.
Dec 1 st at each end of next and every foll 6th row until 16 sts rem, then on foll 5th row. 14 sts.
Work 1 row, ending with **WS** facing for next row.

Shape head

Inc 1 st at each end of next and foll 2 alt rows, ending with RS facing for next row. 20 sts.

Front only

Using the *intarsia* technique, join in a short length of yarn B and work mouth as follows:
Next row (RS) Using yarn A K9, using yarn B K2, using yarn A K9.
Next row Using yarn A P8, using yarn B P1, using yarn A P2, using yarn B P1, using yarn A P8.
Break off yarn B and cont using yarn A only.
Work 6 rows.

Back only

Work 8 rows.

Front and back

Dec 1 st at each end of next and foll 3 alt rows, then on foll 3 rows, ending with RS facing for next row.
Bind off rem 6 sts.

LEGS Ⓑ (make 2)

Using size 2 (2.75mm) needles and yarn A, cast on 12 sts.
Beg with a K row, work in St st as follows:
Work 40 rows, ending with RS facing for next row.

Shape foot

Next row (RS) K9 and turn.
Next row P6 and turn.
Work 12 rows more on these 6 sts only, ending with RS facing for next row.
Next row (RS) K6, then K rem 3 sts.
Bind off all 12 sts purlwise (on **WS**).

ARMS Ⓒ (make 2)

Using size 2 (2.75mm) needles and yarn A, cast on 8 sts.
Beg with a K row, work in St st as follows:
Work 32 rows, ending with RS facing for next row.

Shape thumb

Next row (RS) K5 and turn.
Next row P2 and turn.

chart 1

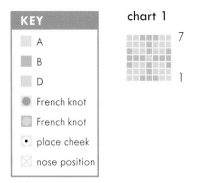

7

1

chart 2

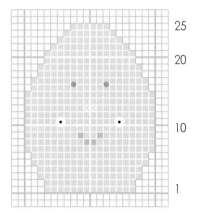

25

20

10

1

Work 4 rows more on these 2 sts only, ending with RS facing for next row.
Next row (RS) K2, then K rem 3 sts.
Next row P8.

Shape hand
Dec 1 st at each end of next and foll alt row, then on foll row. 2 sts.
Next row (RS) K2tog and fasten off.

NOSE
Using size 2 (2.75mm) needles and yarn A, cast on 3 sts.
Beg with a K row, work in St st for 7 rows, ending with **WS** facing for next row.
Bind off purlwise (on **WS**).

CHEEKS (make 2)
Using size C/2 (2.50mm) crochet hook and yarn B, ch5.
Row 1 (RS) 1sc into 2nd ch from hook, 1sc into each of next 3ch.
Fasten off.

FINISHING
Press pieces carefully on WS, using a warm iron over a damp cloth.

Sew together body pieces using backstitch, or mattress stitch if preferred, leaving a small opening. Insert toy filling and sew opening closed. Sew leg and foot seams, leaving cast-on (upper) edge open. Insert toy filling, then sew upper edge closed. Sew across foot near bound-off edge to form heel. Sew upper edges to base of body. Sew arm and thumb seams, leaving cast-on (upper) edge open. Insert a little toy filling, then sew upper edge closed. Sew upper edges to body just below head shaping.

Run gathering threads around outer edge of nose and pull up to form a small ball shape. Using chart 2 as a guide, sew nose to face above mouth. Sew together ends of cheek strips, then gather up inner (foundation-ch) edge so that cheeks form a tiny circle. Using chart 2 as a guide, sew cheeks to face, and embroider French knots for eyes using yarn C.

To form hair, cut 6in [15cm] lengths of yarn C. Lay these lengths on head, starting at top head seam and running over back of head for about 1½in [3.5cm]. Backstitch these lengths in place, sewing through all layers centrally down back of head. Wrap lengths of yarn around hair about 1¼in [3cm] from ends to form pigtails, then attach pigtails to sides of head. Cut ribbon into two equal lengths and tie around pigtails as in photograph. For bangs, cut 2½in [6cm] lengths of yarn C. Wrap another length of yarn around center of these lengths, then attach to center front of head seam as in photograph.

PANTIES
BACK
Using size 2 (2.75mm) needles and yarn B, cast on 11 sts.
Beg with a K row, work in St st as follows:
Work 1 row.
Inc 1 st at each end of next 7 rows, then on foll 2 alt rows, then on foll row, ending with **WS** facing

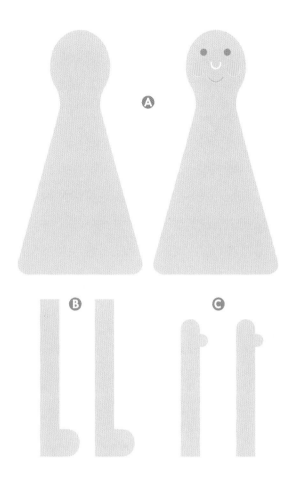

for next row. 31 sts.
Work 2 rows.
Dec 1 st at each end of next row. 29 sts.
Work 1 row, ending with **WS** facing for
next row.
Bind off purlwise (on **WS**).

FRONT
Using size 2 (2.75mm) needles and yarn B, cast
on 11 sts.
Beg with a K row, work in St st as follows:
Work 4 rows, ending with RS facing for next row.
Inc 1 st at each end of next and foll alt row, then
on foll 2 rows, ending with **WS** facing for next
row. 19 sts.

Place flower motif
Using the *intarsia* technique, place flower motif

chart, which is worked entirely in St st beg with a
P row, as follows:
Row 1 (WS) Inc in first st, P5, work next 7 sts as
row 1 of chart 1, P5, inc in last st. 21 sts.
Row 2 Inc in first st, K6, work next 7 sts as row 2
of chart 1, K6, inc in last st. 23 sts.
These 2 rows set position of flower motif chart.
Keeping chart patt correct, inc 1 st at each end
of next row, **2** sts (by inc *twice* in first and last
sts) at each end of foll row, then 1 st at each end
of next row. 31 sts.
Work 1 row.
Dec 1 st at each end of next row, completing
chart row 7. 29 sts.
Break off yarn D and cont using yarn B *only*.
Work 1 row, ending with **WS** facing for
next row.
Bind off purlwise (on **WS**).

FINISHING
Press pieces carefully on WS, using a warm iron
over a damp cloth.

Sew side and crotch seams using backstitch, or
mattress stitch if preferred. Using photograph as
a guide and yarn D, embroider French knot at
center of flower motif on front.

Crochet edging
With RS facing, using size C/2 (2.50mm) crochet
hook and yarn D, attach yarn at top of one side
seam and work around upper edge as follows:
*1sc into edge, ch1, rep from * to end, join with
a slip st to first sc.
Fasten off.
Work crochet edging around leg holes in
same way.

TOP
BACK
Using size 2 (2.75mm) needles and yarn B, cast
on 29 sts.
Beg with a K row, work in St st as follows:
Work 9 rows.
Dec 1 st at each end of next and foll 6th row.
25 sts.
Work 5 rows, ending with **WS** facing for
next row.

Shape armholes

Dec 1 st at each end of next 3 rows. 19 sts.

Work 2 rows, ending with RS facing for next row.

Shape back neck

Next row (RS) K5 and turn.

Work each side of neck separately.

Dec 1 st at neck edge of next 2 rows. 3 sts.

Work 2 rows more, ending with **WS** facing for next row.

Bind off purlwise (on **WS**).

With RS facing, rejoin yarn to rem sts, bind off center 9 sts, K to end. 5 sts.

Complete to match first side, reversing shapings.

FRONT

Using size 2 (2.75mm) needles and yarn B, cast on 29 sts.

Beg with a K row, work in St st as follows:
Work 9 rows.

Dec 1 st at each end of next row. 27 sts.

Work 5 rows, ending with **WS** facing for next row.

Place flower motif

Using the *intarsia* technique, place flower motif chart, which is worked entirely in St st beg with a P row, as follows:

Row 1 (WS) P2tog, P8, work next 7 sts as row 1 of chart 1, P8, P2tog. 25 sts.

Row 2 K9, work next 7 sts as row 2 of chart 1, K9.

These 2 rows set position of flower motif chart.

Working rem 5 rows of flower motif chart and then completing front using yarn B only, cont as follows:

Work 4 rows, ending with **WS** facing for next row.

Shape armholes

Dec 1 st at each end of next 3 rows, ending with RS facing for next row. 19 sts.

Shape front neck

Next row (RS) K7 and turn.

Work each side of neck separately.

Dec 2 sts (by working 3 sts tog) at neck edge of next row. 5 sts.

Dec 1 st at neck edge of next and foll alt row. 3 sts.

Work 2 rows more, ending with **WS** facing for next row.

Bind off purlwise (on **WS**).
With RS facing, rejoin yarn to rem sts, bind off
center 5 sts, K to end. 7 sts.
Complete to match first side, reversing shapings.

FINISHING

Press pieces carefully on WS, using a warm iron
over a damp cloth.

Sew side and shoulder seams using backstitch, or
mattress stitch if preferred. Using photograph as
a guide and yarn D, embroider French knot at
center of flower motif on front.

Crochet edging

With RS facing, using size C/2 (2.50mm) crochet
hook and yarn D, attach yarn at base of one
side seam and work around lower edge as
follows: *1sc into edge, ch1, rep from * to end,
join with a slip st to first sc.
Fasten off.
Work crochet edging around neck and armholes
in same way.

LULA'S DRESS & SHOES

Lula loves this dress because it has flowers on it. She always feels like dancing and singing when she wears it.

BEFORE YOU BEGIN

YARN
To fit Lula Doll

Rowan 4-ply Cotton
B Pink (120)	1 x 50g/1¾oz
C Mauve (130)	1 x 50g/1¾oz
D Pale green (131)	1 x 50g/1¾oz

Note: For the alternative colorways, use B, C, and D where shown in the photographs.

NEEDLES & HOOK
1 pair of size 2 (2.75mm) needles.
Size C/2 (2.50mm) crochet hook.

BUTTONS
1

GAUGE
29 sts and 38 rows = 4in [10cm] square measured over St st using size 2 (2.75mm) needles.

GETTING STARTED

DRESS
BACK
Using size 2 (2.75mm) needles and yarn C, cast on 44 sts.

Row 1 (RS) Knit.
Row 2 Purl.
Row 3 *(P2tog) twice, (M1, K1) 3 times, M1, (P2tog) twice, rep from * to end.
Row 4 Purl.
Rows 5 to 7 Rep rows 1 to 3.
Row 8 P21, P2tog, P21. 43 sts.
Row 9 K2tog, K to last 2 sts, K2tog. 41 sts.

Place chart
Using the *intarsia* technique, work 18 rows foll chart 1, which is worked entirely in St st beg with a *purl* row (chart row 1) and *at same time* dec

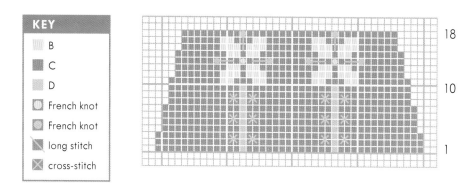

KEY	
	B
	C
	D
	French knot
	French knot
	long stitch
	cross-stitch

1 st at each end of 4th and every foll 4th row, ending with RS facing for next row. 33 sts.
Break off contrasts and cont using yarn C only.
Beg with a K row, work in St st for 4 rows, dec 1 st at each end of 2nd of these rows. 31 sts.
Row 1 (RS) Purl.
Row 2 Purl.
These 2 rows form patt.**
Cont in patt, dec 1 st at each end of next and foll 4th row. 27 sts.
Work 1 row, ending with **RS** facing for next row.

Divide for back opening
Next row (RS) P13 and turn.
Work each side of neck separately.
Dec 1 st at side seam edge of next and foll 3rd row, then on foll row. 10 sts.
Work 4 rows more, ending with RS facing for next row.

Shape neck
Next row (RS) P6, bind off rem 4 sts. 6 sts.
Rejoin yarn with **WS** facing and P to end.
Dec 2 sts (by working 3 sts tog) at neck edge of next row. 4 sts.
Work 2 rows more.
Bind off purlwise (on **WS**).
With RS facing, rejoin yarn to rem sts, P2tog, P to end. 13 sts.
Complete to match first side, reversing shapings.

FRONT
Work as given for back to **.
Cont in patt, dec 1 st at each end of next and every foll 4th row to 25 sts, then on foll 3rd row, then on foll row. 21 sts.

Work 2 rows more, ending with **WS** facing for next row.

Shape neck
Next row (WS) P6 and turn.
Work each side of neck separately.
Dec 1 st at neck edge of next and foll alt row. 4 sts.
Work 2 rows more.
Bind off purlwise (on **WS**).
With **WS** facing, rejoin yarn to rem sts, bind off center 9 sts, P to end. 6 sts.
Complete to match first side, reversing shapings.

FINISHING
Press pieces carefully on WS, using a warm iron over a damp cloth.

Sew side and shoulder seams using backstitch, or mattress stitch if preferred. Using chart as a guide and yarn D, embroider cross-stitches at each side of flower stems, and straight stitches and French knots between flower petals. Using yarn B, embroider French knots at centers of flowers.

Lower edging
With RS facing, using size C/2 (2.50mm) crochet hook and yarn C, attach yarn at base of one side seam and work around lower edge as follows: *1sc into edge, ch1, rep from * to end (ensuring the number of ch sps is divisible by 3), join with a slip st to first sc, 1 slip st into first ch. Join in yarn B.
Round 2 (RS) Using yarn B, ch1 (does **not** count as st), 1sc into same ch sp as slip st at end of previous round, *ch1, 1sc into next ch sp, rep from * to end, ch1, join with a slip st to first sc,

1 slip st into first ch.
Join in yarn D.

Round 3 Rep round 2 but using yarn D.
Round 4 Rep round 2 but using yarn C.
Break off yarn C.
Round 5 Rep round 2.
Break off yarn B.
Round 6 Using yarn D, ch1 (does *not* count as st),
1sc into same ch sp as slip st at end of previous
round, *(ch1, 1sc into next ch sp) twice, ch1, (1sc,
ch3, 1sc) all into next ch sp, rep from * to end,
ch1, join with a slip st to first sc. Fasten off.

Armhole edgings (both alike)

With RS facing, using size C/2 (2.50mm) crochet
hook and yarn D, attach yarn at top of one side
seam and work around armhole edge as follows:
*1sc into edge, ch1, rep from * to end (ensuring
the number of ch sps is divisible by 3), join with a
slip st to first sc, 1 slip st into first ch.
Round 2 (RS) Ch1 (does *not* count as st), 1sc
into same ch sp as slip st at end of previous
round, *(ch1, 1sc into next ch sp) twice, ch1, (1sc,
ch3, 1sc) all into next ch sp, rep from * to end,
ch1, join with a slip st to first sc.
Fasten off.

Neck and back opening edging

With RS facing, using size C/2 (2.50mm) crochet
hook and yarn D, attach yarn at top of right
back opening edge and work around back
opening and neck edge as follows: *1sc into
edge, ch1, rep from * to end (ensuring the
number of ch sps around neck edge is divisible
by 3 plus 1), join with a slip st to first sc, 1 slip st
into first ch.
Round 2 (RS) Ch1 (does *not* count as st), 1sc
into same ch sp as slip st at end of previous
round, *ch1, 1sc into next ch sp, rep from * until
sc has been worked just below left back neck
corner, ch5, 1sc into same ch sp as just worked
into—this forms button loop, now work around
neck edge as follows: ch1, (1sc, ch3, 1sc) all into
next ch sp, **(ch1, 1sc into next ch sp) twice, ch1,
(1sc, ch3, 1sc) all into next ch sp, rep from ** to
end, ch1, join with a slip st to first sc. Fasten off.
Sew on button.

SHOES

MAIN SECTION (make one for each shoe)

Using size 2 (2.75mm) needles and yarn D, cast
on 6 sts.
Working in g st throughout, cont as follows:
Inc 1 st at each end of 2nd and foll 2 alt rows.
12 sts.
Work 1 row.
Dec 1 st at each end of next and foll 2 alt rows,
ending with RS facing for next row. 6 sts.
This section forms sole.

Shape upper

Cast on 4 sts (for heel) at beg of next row.
10 sts.
Inc 1 st at beg (toe edge) of next and foll 2 alt
rows, ending with RS facing for next row. 13 sts.
Bind off 7 sts (for foot opening) at beg of next
row. 6 sts.
Work 3 rows, ending with RS facing for next row.
Cast on 7 sts (for other side of foot opening) at
beg of next row. 13 sts.
Dec 1 st at beg (toe edge) of next and foll 2 alt
rows, ending with RS facing for next row.
Bind off rem 10 sts.

FINISHING

Do *not* press.

Sew heel seams using backstitch, or mattress
stitch if preferred, then sew seam around sole.

Ankle strap

With RS facing and leaving a long end, using
size 2 (2.75mm) needles and yarn D, cast on 4 sts,
then pick up and knit 4 sts across back of main
section—2 sts at each side of heel seam. 8 sts.
Cast on 4 sts at beg of next row. 12 sts.
Knit 2 rows.
Bind off, leaving last st on needle.

Ties

Slip last st of ankle strap onto size C/2 (2.50mm)
crochet hook and ch20.
Fasten off.
Rejoin yarn to long end at other edge of ankle
strap and make other tie in same way.

NIGHTCAP

So soft and gentle, this cute nightcap with its colorful tassle will keep you cozy all night long.

YARN

To fit		2-3 yrs	3-4 yrs	4-5 yrs
Width around head		16½in	17½in	18½in
		42cm	44cm	47cm

Rowan RYC Cashsoft DK and Cashsoft Baby DK

A DK Gray (518)		1	1	1 x 50g/1¾oz
B Baby DK Pale green (804)		1	1	1 x 50g/1¾oz
C DK Orange (510)		small amount for all sizes		

Note: For the alternative colorways, substitute DK Lime green (509), DK Pale mauve (501), or Baby DK Pale blue (805) for both B and C.

NEEDLES

1 pair of size 6 (4mm) needles.

GAUGE

22 sts and 30 rows = 4in [10cm] square measured over pattern using size 6 (4mm) needles.

HAT

Using size 6 (4mm) needles and yarn A, cast on 91 (97: 103) sts.
Cont in patt as follows:
Row 1 (RS) Using yarn A, purl.
Row 2 Using yarn A, knit.
Row 3 Using yarn B, knit.
Row 4 Using yarn B, purl.
These 4 rows form patt.
Cont in patt until hat meas 5 (5½: 6)in [13 (14: 15)cm], ending after patt row 2 and with RS facing for next row.

Shape top

Keeping patt correct, cont as follows:
Row 1 (RS) *K13 (14: 15), K2tog, rep from * to last st, K1. 85 (91: 97) sts.
Work 3 rows.
Row 5 *K12 (13: 14), K2tog, rep from * to last st, K1. 79 (85: 91) sts.
Work 3 rows.
Row 9 *K11 (12: 13), K2tog, rep from * to last st, K1. 73 (79: 85) sts.
Work 3 rows.
Row 13 *K10 (11: 12), K2tog, rep from * to last st, K1. 67 (73: 79) sts.
Work 3 rows.
Row 17 *K9 (10: 11),

K2tog, rep from * to last st, K1. 61 (67: 73) sts.
Work 3 rows.
Cont in this way, decreasing 6 sts on next and every foll 4th row until the foll row has been worked:

Next row (K2tog) 6 times, K1. 7 sts.
Work 3 rows.
Next row K2tog, K3tog, K2tog.
Next row P3tog and fasten off.

TASSEL STRIP

Using size 6 (4mm) needles and yarn C, cast on 4 sts.
Beg with a K row, work in St st for 4 rows, ending with RS facing for next row.
Break off yarn C and join in yarn A.
Cont in St st until tassel strip meas 4½ in [11cm], ending with RS facing for next row. Bind off.

FINISHING

Press pieces carefully on WS, using a warm iron over a damp cloth.

Sew together row-end edges of tassel strip. Using yarn C, make a 2in [5cm] long tassel and attach to cast-on edge of tassel strip. Sew back seam of hat, enclosing bound-off edge of tassel strip in seam at top of hat.

BEDTIME BATHROBE

Warm and comfortable, the Bedtime Bathrobe is a must-have for all boys. Try counting the numbers on the pockets to send yourself to sleep.

YARN

Sizes	2-3 yrs	3-4 yrs	4-5 yrs
To fit chest	22in	24in	26in
	56cm	61cm	66cm
Actual size	26in	28¼in	30¼in
	66cm	72cm	77cm
Back length	20in	22in	23½in
	51cm	56cm	60cm
Underarm seam	9in	10½in	12¼in
	23cm	27cm	31cm

Rowan RYC Cashsoft DK and Cashsoft Baby DK

A DK Gray (518)	6	7	8 x 50g/1¾oz
B Baby DK Pale green (804)	1	1	1 x 50g/1¾oz
C DK Orange (510)	1	1	1 x 50g/1¾oz

NEEDLES & HOOK
1 pair of size 6 (4mm) needles.
Size E/4 (3.50mm) crochet hook.

BUTTONS
2

GAUGE
22 sts and 30 rows = 4in [10cm] square measured over St st using size 6 (4mm) needles.

RIGHT FRONT
Using size 6 (4mm) needles and yarn A, cast on 46 (49: 52) sts.
Row 1 (RS) K2, *P1, K3, rep from * to last 0 (3: 2) sts, P0 (1: 1), K0 (2: 1).
Row 2 K1 (0: 0), P1 (1: 0), *K3, P1, rep from * to end.
These 2 rows form fancy rib.
Work 6 rows more in fancy rib, ending with RS facing for next row.
Beg with a K row, work in St st, shaping side seam by dec 1 st at end of 9th and every foll 8th

(10th: 12th) row until 37 (40: 43) sts rem.
Work 15 (11: 5) rows more, ending with RS facing for next row. Right front should now meas 12½ (14: 15¼)in [32 (36: 39)cm].
Next row (RS) K2, *P1, K3, rep from * to last 3 (2: 1) sts, P1, K2 (1: 0).
Next row K0 (0: 2), P1 (0: 1), *K3, P1, rep from * to end.
These 2 rows form fancy rib.
Cont in fancy rib until right front meas 1½in [4cm] **from beg of fancy rib**, ending with **WS** facing for next row.

Shape sleeve
Keeping patt correct, cast on 11 (10: 9) sts at beg of next row, then 10 sts at beg of foll 4 (5: 6) alt rows. 88 (100: 112) sts.
Work even until right front meas 19¼ (21¼: 22¾)in [49 (54: 58)cm], ending with RS facing for next row.

Shape neck
Next row (RS) Patt 17 (18: 19) sts and slip these sts onto a holder, patt to end. 71 (82: 93) sts.
Work 6 rows, ending with **WS** facing for next row.
Place marker at end of last row.
Work 1 row, ending with RS facing for next row.
Cast on 3 sts at beg of next row, then 4 sts at beg of foll alt row. 78 (89: 100) sts.
Work 1 row, ending with RS facing for next row.
Break off yarn and leave sts on a holder.

LEFT FRONT
Using size 6 (4mm) needles and yarn A, cast on 46 (49: 52) sts.
Row 1 (RS) K0 (2: 1), P0 (1: 1), *K3, P1, rep from * to last 2 sts, K2.
Row 2 *P1, K3, rep from * to last 2 (1: 0) sts, P1 (1: 0), K1 (0: 0).
These 2 rows form fancy rib.

chart 1

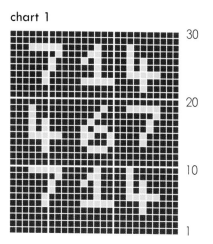

KEY
- ■ A
- □ B
- ● French knot
- ╱ long stitch
- ◥ long stitch

chart 2

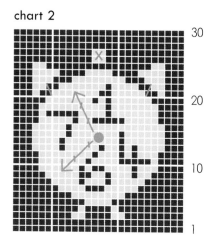

Work 6 rows more in fancy rib, ending with RS facing for next row.

Beg with a K row, work in St st, shaping side seam by dec 1 st at beg of 9th and every foll 8th (10th: 12th) row until 37 (40: 43) sts rem.

Work 15 (11: 5) rows more, ending with RS facing for next row.

Next row (RS) K2 (1: 0), P1, *K3, P1, rep from * to last 2 sts, K2.

Next row *P1, K3, rep from * to last 1 (0: 3) sts, P1 (0: 1), K0 (0: 2).

These 2 rows form fancy rib.

Cont in fancy rib until 1 row less has been worked than on right front to beg of sleeve shaping, ending with RS facing for next row.

Shape sleeve

Keeping patt correct, cast on 11 (10: 9) sts at beg of next row, then 10 sts at beg of foll 4 (5: 6) alt rows. 88 (100: 112) sts.

Work even until left front matches right front to beg of neck shaping, ending with RS facing for next row.

Shape neck

Next row (RS) Patt to last 17 (18: 19) sts and turn, leaving rem sts on a holder. 71 (82: 93) sts.

Work 6 rows, ending with **WS** facing for next row. Place marker at beg of last row.

Work 2 rows, ending with **WS** facing for next row.

Cast on 3 sts at beg of next row, then 4 sts at beg of foll alt row, ending with RS facing for next row. 78 (89: 100) sts.

Do **not** break off yarn.

BACK

With RS facing and using size 6 (4mm) needles, join left and right fronts as follows:

Next row (RS) Patt across 78 (89: 100) sts of left front, cast on 19 (21: 23) sts onto right needle, patt across 78 (89: 100) sts of right front. 175 (199: 223) sts.

Cont in fancy rib across all sts until work meas same from markers as from last sleeve cast-on sts to markers, ending with RS facing for next row.

Shape sleeves

Keeping patt correct, bind off 10 sts at beg of next 8 (10: 12) rows, then 11 (10: 9) sts at beg of foll 2 rows. 73 (79: 85) sts.

Work even until back meas 1½in [4cm] **from last set of bound-off sts**, ending with RS facing for next row.

Beg with a K row, work in St st, inc 1 st at each end of 17th (13th: 7th) and every foll 8th (10th: 12th) row until there are 91 (97: 103) sts.

Work 7 rows more, ending with RS facing for next row.

Next row (RS) K0 (2: 1), P0 (1: 1), *K3, P1, rep from * to last 3 (2: 1) sts, K3 (2: 1).

Next row K1 (0: 3), *P1, K3, rep from * to last 2 (1: 0) sts, P1 (1: 0), K1 (0: 0).

These 2 rows form fancy rib.

Work 6 rows more in fancy rib, ending with RS facing for next row.

Bind off in fancy rib.

LEFT POCKET

Using size 6 (4mm) needles and yarn A, cast on 26 sts.

Using the *intarsia* technique, work 30 rows foll chart 2 for clock, which is worked entirely in St st beg with a K row (chart row 1), ending with RS facing for next row.

Break off contrasts and cont using yarn C only. Purl 2 rows, ending with RS facing for next row.

Beg with a K row, work in St st for 8 rows, ending with RS facing for next row. Bind off.

RIGHT POCKET

Work as given for left pocket, but foll chart 1 for numbers.

FINISHING

Press pieces carefully on WS, using a warm iron over a damp cloth.

Sew both shoulder seams using backstitch, or mattress stitch if preferred.

COLLAR

With RS facing, using size 6 (4mm) needles and yarn A, slip 17 (18: 19) sts from right front holder onto right needle, rejoin yarn and pick up and knit 47 (49: 51) sts around neck shaping, then patt across 17 (18: 19) sts from left front holder. 81 (85: 89) sts.

Work in fancy rib as set by sts left on holders for 3in [8cm], ending with RS facing for next row. Bind off in fancy rib.

Sew side and sleeve seams.

Using yarn C and chart 2 as a guide, embroider hands onto the clock of left pocket, securing the long strands with short couching stitches; then work two short sts to form point at ends. Using yarn C, embroider a French knot at center of clock face, a short straight st at each side to connect bells to clock, then a cross-stitch centrally on hammer section at top. Fold last 9 rows to WS across top of pockets, then using photograph as a guide, sew pockets to fronts.

Right front edging

With RS facing, using size E/4 (3.50mm) crochet hook and yarn A, attach yarn at cast-on edge of right front opening edge and work 1 row of sc up right front opening edge to top of collar. Fasten off.

Mark positions for two buttons along this edge—first to come at start of fancy rib yoke, second to come 1½in [4cm] above.

Left front edging

With RS facing, using size E/4 (3.50mm) crochet hook and yarn A, attach yarn at top of collar and work 1 row of sc down left front opening edge to cast-on edge, making buttonholes to correspond with positions marked for buttons by working enough chains to fit button. Fasten off.

Sew on buttons.

BEDTIME SOCKS

Bedtime Socks are a comfortable and stylish accessory for the Bedtime Bathrobe. Everyone will want to wear them!

YARN

To fit	2-3 yrs	3-4 yrs	4-5 yrs
Length of foot	5¼in	5¾in	6in
	13.5cm	14.5cm	15.5cm

Rowan RYC Cashsoft DK and Cashsoft Baby DK			
A DK Gray (518)	1	1	1 x 50g/1¾oz
B DK Orange (510)	1	1	1 x 50g/1¾oz
C Baby DK Pale green (804)	1	1	1 x 50g/1¾oz

NEEDLES

1 pair each of size 3 (3.25mm) and size 6 (4mm) needles.

GAUGE

22 sts and 30 rows = 4in [10cm] square measured over St st using size 6 (4mm) needles.

SOCKS (make 2)

Using size 3 (3.25mm) needles and yarn B, cast on 37 sts.
Break off yarn B and join in yarn A.
Row 1 (RS) P1, *K3, P1, rep from * to end.
Row 2 K2, *P1, K3, rep from * to last 3 sts, P1, K2.
These 2 rows form rib.
Work in rib until sock meas 3½in [9cm], dec 1 st at end of last row and ending with RS facing for next row. 36 sts.

Shape top of foot

Break off yarn.
Slip first 9 sts and last 9 sts onto holders.
With RS facing and using size 6 (4mm) needles, rejoin yarn A to center 18 sts and cont in St st, beg with a K row, as follows:
Using yarn A, work 2 rows.
Using yarn C, work 2 rows.
These 4 rows form striped St st.

Work 22 (24: 28) rows more in striped St st, ending with RS facing for next row.

Shape toe

Next row (RS) K2, sl 1, K1, psso, K to last 4 sts, K2tog, K1.
Next row P2, P2tog, P to last 4 sts, P2tog tbl, P2.
Rep last 2 rows twice more. 6 sts.
Next row (RS) (K2tog) 3 times.
Bind off rem 3 sts (on **WS**).

Shape heel

Slip the two sets of 9 sts from holders onto a size 6 (4mm) needle, with row-end edges meeting at center. Rejoin yarn B to these 18 sts with RS facing and cont as follows:
Beg with a K row, work 10 rows in St st, ending with RS facing for next row.

Turn heel

Row 1 (RS) K9, K2tog tbl, K1 and turn.
Row 2 Sl 1, P1, P2tog, P1 and turn.
Row 3 Sl 1, K2, K2tog tbl, K1 and turn.
Row 4 Sl 1, P3, P2tog, P1 and turn.
Row 5 Sl 1, K4, K2tog tbl, K1 and turn.
Row 6 Sl 1, P5, P2tog, P1 and turn.
Row 7 Sl 1, K6, K2tog tbl, K1 and turn.
Row 8 Sl 1, P7, P2tog, P1. 10 sts.
Break off yarn.
With RS facing, using size 6 (4mm) needles and yarn A, pick up and knit 10 sts along row-end edge of first side of heel, K 10 heel sts, then pick up and knit 10 sts along other side of heel. 30 sts.
Next row Purl.
Join in yarn C.
Beg with 2 rows using yarn C, cont in striped St st as given for top of foot as follows:
Next row (RS) K2, sl 1, K1, psso, K to last 4 sts, K2tog, K2.
Next row Purl.
Rep last 2 rows 5 times more. 18 sts.

Work 12 (14: 18) rows more, ending with RS
facing for next row.
Complete as given for top of foot from beg of
toe shaping.

FINISHING

Press pieces carefully on WS, using a warm iron
over a damp cloth.

Sew heel seam. Sew foot and toe seams.

FLORIAN FOX

Florian Fox loves to run about at night under the stars. His scarf will keep him warm as he gets up to no good.

BEFORE YOU BEGIN

YARN

Size of toy	7½ x 17in [19 x 43cm]

Rowan RYC Cashsoft DK and Cashsoft Baby DK

A DK Gray (518)	2 x 50g/1¾oz
B Baby DK Pale green (804)	1 x 50g/1¾oz
C DK Pale blue (503)	1 x 50g/1¾oz
D DK Lime green (509)	1 x 50g/1¾oz

Note: For the orange scarf, use DK Orange (510) for D—instead of DK Lime green (509).

NEEDLES

1 pair of size 6 (4mm) needles.

EXTRAS

Washable toy filling.

GAUGE

22 sts and 30 rows = 4in [10cm] square measured over St st using size 6 (4mm) needles.

GETTING STARTED

RIGHT SIDE A

Back leg

Using size 6 (4mm) needles and yarn A, cast on 5 sts.
Beg with a K row, work in St st as follows:
Work 1 row.
Row 2 (WS) Inc once in each of first 2 sts, P1, inc once in each of last 2 sts. 9 sts.
Row 3 Inc in first st, K to last 2 sts, inc once in each of last 2 sts. 12 sts.
Work 3 rows, ending with RS facing for next row.
Dec 1 st at beg of next row and at same edge on foll 2 rows. 9 sts.
Work 13 rows, ending with RS facing for next row.**
Break off yarn and leave sts on a holder.

Front leg

Work as given for back leg to **.

Join legs

Next row (RS) K 9 sts of front leg, cast on 19 sts onto right needle, K 9 sts of back leg. 37 sts.***
Using the *intarsia* technique, work foll chart 1 (see page 36), which is worked entirely in St st beg with a **purl** row (chart row 1), as follows:
Keeping chart patt correct, inc 1 st at end of next row (chart row 1) and at same edge on next and foll alt row.
Work 1 row, ending with RS facing for next row. 40 sts.
Cast on 3 sts at beg of next row and 4 sts at beg of 2 foll alt rows, then 3 sts at beg of foll alt row.
Work 1 row, ending with RS facing for next row. 54 sts.
Cast on 2 sts at beg of next and foll alt row.
Inc 1 st at shaped edge of next 2 rows, then on foll 5 alt rows, then on foll 4th row. 66 sts.
Work 3 rows, ending with RS facing for next row.
Bind off.

LEFT SIDE B

Work as given for right side, reversing all shaping by reversing RS of work by reading K for P and vice versa, and foll chart 2.

UNDERBODY C

Work as given for right side to ***.
Using the *intarsia* technique, work foll chart 3, which is worked entirely in St st beg with a **purl** row, as follows:
Chart row 1 (WS) Using A, purl.
Keeping chart patt correct, cast on 2 sts at beg of next row, inc 1 st at same edge on foll alt row, then cast on 3 sts at beg of foll alt row. Work 1 row, ending with RS facing for next row. 43 sts.
Cast on 4 sts at beg of next and foll alt row. 51 sts.
Work 1 row.

chart 1

place ears here

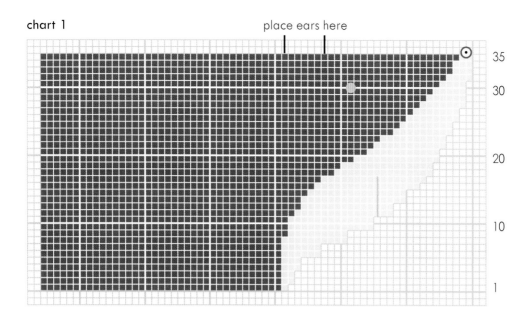

35
30
20
10
1

chart 2

place ears here

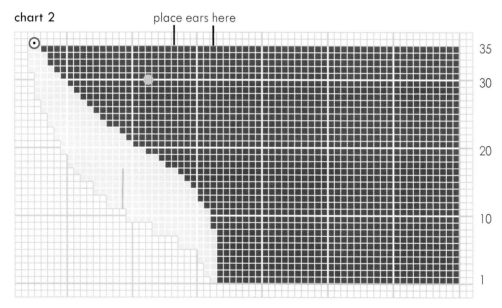

35
30
20
10
1

chart 3

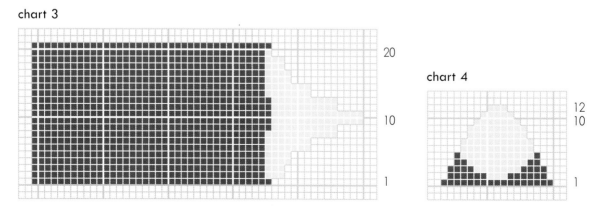

20
10
1

chart 4

12
10
1

KEY

- A
- B
- C
- ⊙ French knot
- ╲ long stich
- • place nose

Bind off 4 sts at beg of next and foll alt row. 43 sts.

Bind off 3 sts at beg of next alt row, dec 1 st at beg of foll alt row and bind off 2 sts at beg of next alt row, ending with **WS** facing for next row.

37 sts.

Cont in St st, beg with a P row and using yarn A only as follows:

Work 1 row.

Shape front leg

Next row (RS) K9 and turn, leaving rem sts on a holder.

****Work 14 rows more on these 9 sts, ending with **WS** facing for next row.

Inc 1 st at end of next row and at same edge on foll 2 rows. 12 sts.

Work 3 rows, ending with **WS** facing for next row.

Next row (WS) (P2tog) twice, P to last 2 sts, P2tog. 9 sts.

Next row (K2tog) twice, K1, (K2tog) twice. Bind off rem 5 sts purlwise (on **WS**).

Return to sts left on holder, rejoin yarn with RS

facing, bind off center 19 sts, K to end. 9 sts. Complete back leg to match front leg from ****.

TAIL Ⓓ (make 2)

Using size 6 (4mm) needles and yarn A, cast on 13 sts.

Beg with a K row, work in St st as follows:

Work 5 rows, ending with **WS** facing for next row.

Inc 1 st at each end of next and foll 3rd row, then on foll 2 alt rows. 21 sts.

Work 9 rows, ending with RS facing for next row.

Dec 1 st at each end of next and foll 4th row, ending with WS facing for next row. 17 sts.

Using the *intarsia* technique, work foll chart 4, which is worked entirely in St st beg with a **purl** row, as follows:

Chart row 1 (WS) Using A, purl.

Keeping chart patt correct, dec 1 st at each end of next and foll 4 alt rows, then on foll 2 rows, ending with **WS** facing for next row.

Bind off rem 3 sts purlwise (on **WS**).

OUTER EARS Ⓔ (make 2)

Using size 6 (4mm) needles and yarn A, cast on 15 sts.

Beg with a K row, work in St st as follows:

Work 4 rows, ending with RS facing for next row.

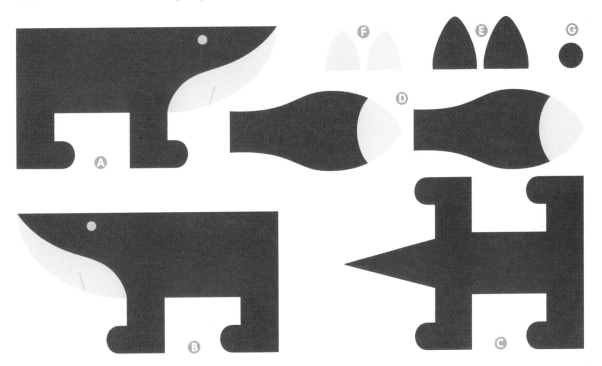

Row 5 (RS) K1, sl 1, K1, psso, K to last 3 sts, K2tog, K1.

Row 6 Purl.

Rep rows 5 and 6 four times more. 5 sts.

Row 15 (RS) K1, sl 1, K2tog, psso, K1.

Row 16 P3.

Row 17 Sl 1, K2tog, psso and fasten off.

INNER EARS  (make 2)

Using size 6 (4mm) needles and yarn B, cast on 11 sts.

Beg with a K row, work in St st as follows:

Work 4 rows, ending with RS facing for next row.

Row 5 (RS) K1, sl 1, K1, psso, K to last 3 sts, K2tog, K1.

Row 6 Purl.

Rep rows 5 and 6 twice more. 5 sts.

Row 11 (RS) K1, sl 1, K2tog, psso, K1.

Row 12 P3.

Row 13 Sl 1, K2tog, psso and fasten off.

NOSE

Using size 6 (4mm) needles and yarn A, cast on 2 sts.

Beg with a K row, work in St st as follows:

Work 2 rows, ending with RS facing for next row.

Row 3 (RS) Inc once in both sts. 4 sts.

Work 3 rows, ending with RS facing for next row.

Row 7 (RS) (K2tog) twice.

Row 8 P2.

Row 9 K2tog and fasten off, leaving a long end.

SCARF

Using size 6 (4mm) needles and yarn D, cast on 12 sts.

Work in g st for 10 rows, ending with RS facing for next row.

Joining in colors as required, cont in patt as follows:

Rows 1 and 2 Using yarn B, purl.

Row 3 (RS) Using yarn C, purl.

Row 4 Using yarn C, knit.

Rows 5 and 6 Rep rows 1 and 2.

Row 7 Using yarn D, purl.

Row 8 Using yarn D, knit.

These 8 rows form patt.

Rep last 8 rows 18 times more.

Using yarn D, work in g st for 8 rows, ending with RS facing for next row. Bind off.

FINISHING

Press pieces carefully on WS, using a warm iron over a damp cloth.

Sew pairs of tail pieces together, leaving cast-on edges open. Insert toy filling. Sew underbody and sides together, matching shaped edges and leaving opening in back seam for tail. Insert toy filling, then sew tail to body. Sew outer ears to inner ears, leaving cast-on edges open. Fold ears in half, then sew to top of head as indicated on chart. Run gathering thread around outer edge of nose and pull up so nose forms a small ball shape. Sew to front of head as indicated on charts. Cut four 2in [5cm] lengths of yarn A and knot two of these lengths through each side of head next to nose to form whiskers. Using charts as a guide and yarn C, embroider French knots for eyes; and for mouth, work three pairs of straight sts radiating out from point where underbody and sides meet. Sew together row-end edges of scarf. Positioning seam centrally along scarf, sew ends closed.

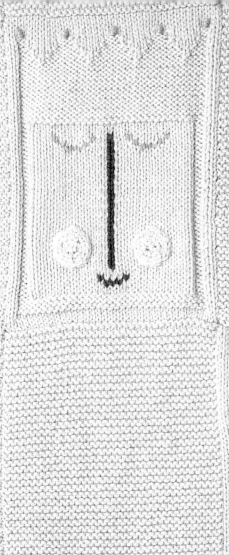
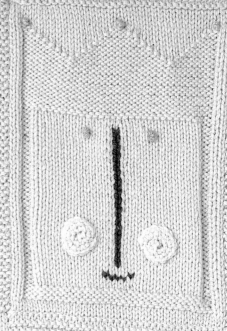
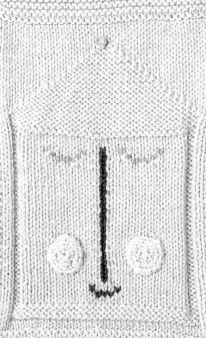
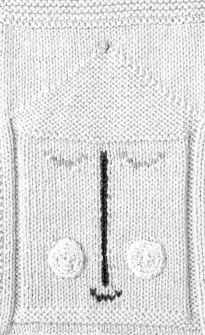
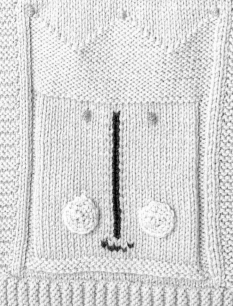
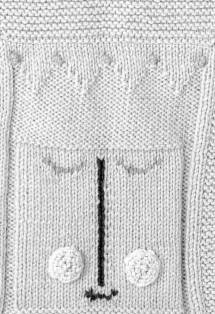

SNOOZE BLANKET

Beautifully warm and soft, this blanket features the "King of Snooze"
winking, blinking, and snoozing. Ssshhh, you may wake him up!

BEFORE YOU BEGIN

YARN

Size of blanket	34¼ x 43in [87 x 109cm]

Rowan RYC Cashsoft Baby DK and Cashsoft DK

A Baby DK Pale green (804)	15 x 50g/1¾ oz
B Baby DK Pink (807)	1 x 50g/1¾ oz
C DK Brown (517)	1 x 50g/1¾ oz
D DK Pale blue (503)	1 x 50g/1¾ oz
E DK Lime green (509)	1 x 50g/1¾ oz

NEEDLES & HOOK

1 pair each of size 5 (3.75mm) and size 6 (4mm)
needles.
Size E/4 (3.50mm) crochet hook.

GAUGE

22 sts and 30 rows = 4in [10cm] square measured
over St st using size 6 (4mm) needles.

GETTING STARTED

PLAIN BLOCK (make 12)

Using size 6 (4mm) needles and yarn A, cast on
37 sts.
Work in g st for 89 rows, ending with **WS** facing
for next row.
Bind off knitwise (on **WS**).

CHEEKS (make 26)

Using size E/4 (3.50mm) crochet hook and yarn B,
ch4 and join with a slip st to form a ring.
Round 1 Ch1 (does *not* count as st), (1sc into
ring, ch1) 5 times, join with a slip st to first sc.
Round 2 Ch1 (does *not* count as st),
1sc into first sc, ch1, 1sc into next
ch sp, ch1, (1sc into next sc, ch1,
1sc into next ch sp, ch1, skip 1sc,
1sc into next ch sp, ch1) twice,
join with a slip st to first sc.
Fasten off.

BLOCK A (make 5)

Using size 6 (4mm) needles and yarn A, cast on 39 sts.

Joining in and breaking off colors as required, using the *intarsia* technique, and beg with chart row 1 (a RS knit row), work 70 rows foll chart A, ending with RS facing for next row.
Bind off.

Sew cheeks over P sts on row 17. Using yarn D, embroider French knot eyes on row 42. Using yarn E, embroider French knots on points of crown on row 66.

BLOCK B (make 4)

Using size 6 (4mm) needles and yarn A, cast on 39 sts.

Joining in and breaking off colors as required, using the *intarsia* technique, and beg with chart row 1 (a RS knit row), work 70 rows foll chart B, ending with RS facing for next row.
Bind off.

Sew cheeks over P sts on row 17. Using yarn E, embroider French knot at top of hat on row 66.

BLOCK C (make 4)

Using size 6 (4mm) needles and yarn A, cast on 39 sts.

Joining in and breaking off colors as required, using the intarsia technique, and beg with chart

chart A

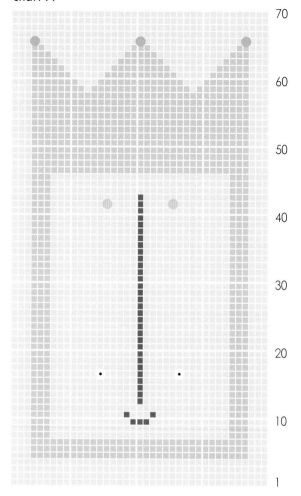

row 1 (a RS knit row), work 70 rows foll chart C, ending with RS facing for next row. Bind off.

Sew cheeks over P sts on row 17. Using yarn E, embroider French knots on points of crown on row 66.

FINISHING

Press pieces carefully on WS, using a warm iron over a damp cloth.

Following diagram on the left, sew together blocks to form one large rectangle.

Side borders (both alike)

Using size 5 (3.75mm) needles and yarn A, cast on 13 sts.

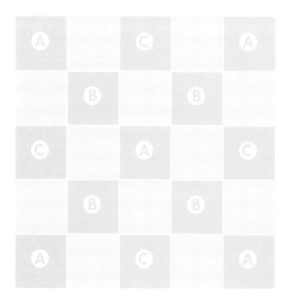

chart B

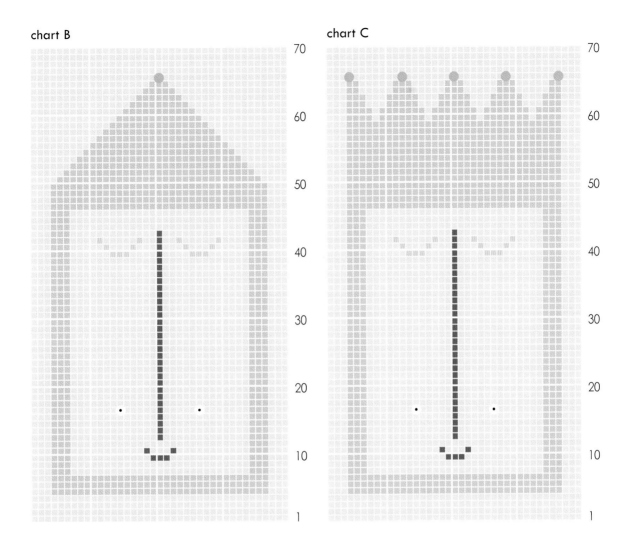

chart C

Row 1 (RS) Purl.
Rows 2 and 3 Knit.
Row 4 Purl.
These 4 rows form patt.
Cont in patt until side border, when slightly
stretched, fits along side edge of joined blocks,
ending with RS facing for next row.
Bind off.

Sew side borders in place.

End borders (both alike)
Using size 5 (3.75mm) needles and yarn A, cast
on 13 sts.
Work in patt as given for side borders until end
border, when slightly stretched, fits along entire
upper (or lower) edge of joined blocks and side
borders, ending with RS facing for next row.
Bind off.

Sew end borders in place.

Press seams
carefully.

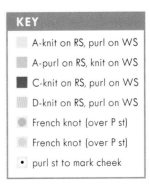

KEY	
	A-knit on RS, purl on WS
	A-purl on RS, knit on WS
	C-knit on RS, purl on WS
	D-knit on RS, purl on WS
	French knot (over P st)
	French knot (over P st)
•	purl st to mark cheek

SNOOZE PJ CASE

There is plenty of room in the Snooze PJ Case for your pajamas or nightie. He complements the Snooze Blanket beautifully.

BEFORE YOU BEGIN

YARN

Size of case   9 x 16in [23 x 41cm]

Rowan RYC Cashsoft Baby DK and Cashsoft DK

A	Baby DK Pale green (804)	2 x 50g/1¾ oz
B	Baby DK Pink (807)	1 x 50g/1¾ oz
C	DK Brown (517)	1 x 50g/1¾ oz
D	DK Pale blue (503)	1 x 50g/1¾ oz
E	DK Lime green (509)	1 x 50g/1¾ oz

NEEDLES & HOOK

1 pair each of size 3 (3.25mm) and size 6 (4mm) needles.
Size E/4 (3.50mm) crochet hook.

BUTTONS

3

GAUGE

22 sts and 30 rows = 4in [10cm] square measured over St st using size 6 (4mm) needles.

GETTING STARTED

BACK

Using size 3 (3.25mm) needles and yarn A, cast on 51 sts.
Row 1 (RS) K1, *P1, K1, rep from * to end.
Row 2 P1, *K1, P1, rep from * to end.
These 2 rows form rib.
Cont in rib for 8 rows more, ending with RS facing for next row.
Change to size 6 (4mm) needles.
Beg with a K row, work in St st for 76 rows, ending with RS facing for next row.

Shape for hat
Row 1 (RS) Using yarn A, purl.
Row 2 Using yarn A, knit.
Join in yarn D.

KEY

▢	A
◼	C
▥	D
•	place cheek

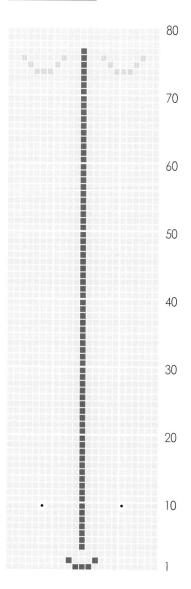

44

45

Row 3 Using yarn D, K2tog, K to last 2 sts, K2tog.

Row 4 Using yarn D, purl.

These 4 rows form patt and beg hat shaping.

Cont in patt, dec 1 st at each end of next and every foll alt row until 3 sts rem.

Work 1 row, ending with RS facing for next row.

Next row (RS) Sl 1, K2tog, psso and fasten off.

FRONT

Using size 3 (3.25mm) needles and yarn A, cast on 51 sts.

Work in rib as given for back for 4 rows, ending with RS facing for next row.

Row 5 (RS) Rib 10, (bind off 3 sts, rib until there are 11 sts on right needle after bind-off) twice, bind off 3 sts, rib to end.

Row 6 Rib to end, casting on 3 sts over those bound off on previous row.

Work 4 rows more in rib, ending with RS facing for next row.

Change to size 6 (4mm) needles.

Beg with a K row, work in St st for 34 rows, ending with RS facing for next row.

Joining in and breaking off colors as required and using the *intarsia* technique, work center 23 sts foll chart, which is worked entirely in St st beg with a K row (chart row 1), until all 80 rows of chart have been completed, ending with RS facing for next row.

Complete as given for back from beg of hat shaping.

CHEEKS (make 2)

Using size E/4 (3.50mm) crochet hook and yarn B, ch4 and join with a slip st to form a ring.

Round 1 Ch1 (does *not* count as st), (1sc into ring, ch1) 5 times, join with a slip st to first sc.

Round 2 Ch1 (does *not* count as st), 1sc into first sc, ch1, 1sc into next ch sp, ch1, (1sc into next sc, ch1, 1sc into next ch sp, ch1, skip 1sc, 1sc into next ch sp, ch1) twice, join with a slip st to first sc.

Fasten off.

Using chart as a guide, sew cheeks to front.

TASSEL STRIP

Using size 6 (4mm) needles and yarn E, cast on 4 sts.
Beg with a K row, work in St st for 4 rows, ending with RS facing for next row.
Break off yarn E and join in yarn A.
Cont in St st until tassel strip meas 4½ in [11cm], ending with RS facing for next row. Bind off.

FINISHING

Press pieces carefully on WS, using a warm iron over a damp cloth.

Sew together row-end edges of tassel strip. Using yarn E, make a 2½ in [6cm] long tassel and attach to cast-on edge of tassel strip. Sew front to back along row-end edges, positioning cast-on edge of back 38 rows above cast-on edge of front and enclosing bound-off edge of tassel strip in seam at top of hat.

Crochet edging

With RS facing, using size E/4 (3.50mm) crochet hook and yarn D, attach yarn at one end of cast-on edge of front and cont as follows: ch1 (does *not* count as st), 1sc into first cast-on st, ch1, skip 2 cast-on sts, *1sc into next cast-on st, ch1, skip 1 cast-on st, rep from * to last 4 sts, 1sc into next cast-on st, ch1, skip 2 cast-on sts, 1sc into last cast-on st.
Fasten off.

Sew on buttons.

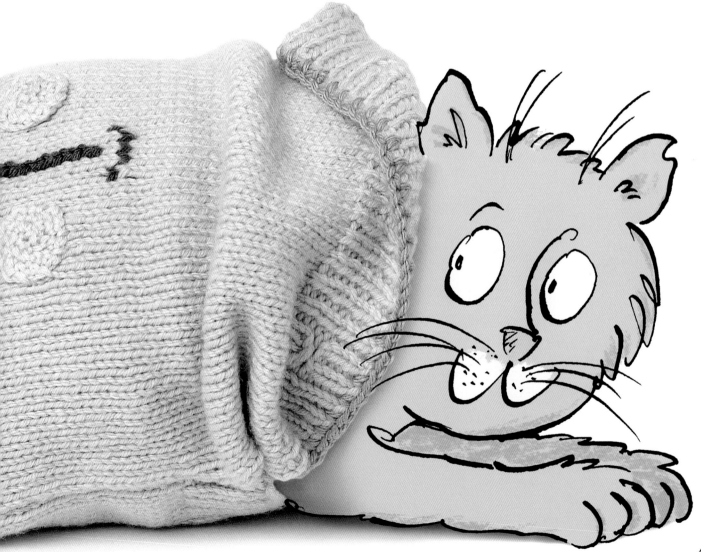

DREAM CARDIGAN

Very, very cozy and very, very sweet, this really is a dream cardigan. The pretty little ribbon makes it even more special.

BEFORE YOU BEGIN

YARN

Sizes	2-3 yrs	3-4 yrs	4-5 yrs
To fit chest	22in	24in	26in
	56cm	61cm	66cm
Actual size	25½in	27in	29in
	65cm	69cm	74cm
Back length	15¾in	17¾in	19¼in
	40cm	45cm	49cm
Underarm seam	5½in	7in	8½in
	14cm	18cm	22cm

Rowan RYC Cashsoft DK			
Pale mauve (501)	8	9	10 x 50g/1¾oz

NEEDLES & HOOK

1 pair each of size 8 (5mm) and size 10½ (7mm) needles.
Size E/4 (3.50mm) crochet hook.

BUTTONS

3

EXTRAS

39in [100cm] of narrow ribbon.

GAUGE

19 sts and 23 rows = 4in [10cm] square measured over pattern using size 8 (5mm) needles and yarn *double*.
17 sts and 20 rows = 4in [10cm] square measured over pattern using size 10½ (7mm) needles and yarn *double*.

GETTING STARTED

BODICE AND SLEEVES (worked in one piece, beg at lower back edge)

Using size 8 (5mm) needles and yarn *double*, cast on 62 (66: 70) sts.
Row 1 (RS) Knit.
Row 2 *P2tog leaving sts on left needle, K tog same 2 sts again and slip sts off left needle, rep from * to end.
Row 3 Knit.
Row 4 P1, *P2tog leaving sts on left needle, K tog same 2 sts again and slip sts off left needle, rep from * to last st, P1.
These 4 rows form patt.
Cont in patt for 6 rows more, ending with RS facing for next row.

Shape for sleeves

Keeping patt correct, cast on 8 sts at beg of next 6 (8: 10) rows. 110 (130: 150) sts.
Cont in patt until work meas 4¾ (5: 5½)in [12 (13: 14)cm] **from beg of sleeve shaping**, ending with RS facing for next row.

Shape neck and right front

Next row (RS) Patt 47 (56: 65) sts and turn, leaving rem sts on a holder.
Work each side of neck separately.
Keeping patt correct, bind off 5 sts at beg of next row. 42 (51: 60) sts.
Dec 1 st at neck edge of next 2 rows. 40 (49: 58) sts.
Place marker at end of last row.
Work 5 rows, ending with **WS** facing for next row.
Inc 1 st at neck edge of next and foll alt row, then on foll 3 rows, ending with **WS** facing for next row. 45 (54: 63) sts.
Cast on 10 (11: 12) sts at beg of next row. 55 (65: 75) sts.
Work even until work meas same **from** marker as from last set of sleeve cast-on sts **to** marker, ending with RS facing for next row.

Shape sleeve

Keeping patt correct, bind off 8 sts at beg of next and foll 2 (3: 4) alt rows. 31 (33: 35) sts.
Work 11 rows more, ending with RS facing for next row. Bind off.

Shape left front

With RS facing, rejoin yarn **double** to rem sts, bind off center 16 (18: 20) sts, patt to end. 47 (56: 65) sts.

Work 1 row.

Keeping patt correct, bind off 5 sts at beg of next row. 42 (51: 60) sts.

Dec 1 st at neck edge of next 2 rows. 40 (49: 58) sts.

Place marker at end of last row.

Work 5 rows, ending with RS facing for next row.

Inc 1 st at neck edge of next and foll alt row, then on foll 3 rows, ending with RS facing for next row. 45 (54: 63) sts.

Cast on 10 (11: 12) sts at beg of next row. 55 (65: 75) sts.

Work even until work meas same **from** marker as from last set of sleeve cast-on sts **to** marker, ending with **WS** facing for next row.

Shape sleeve

Keeping patt correct, bind off 8 sts at beg of next and foll 2 (3: 4) alt rows. 31 (33: 35) sts.

Work 10 rows more, ending with RS facing for next row.

Bind off.

CUFFS (both alike)

With RS facing, using size 8 (5mm) needles and yarn **double**, pick up and knit 42 (46: 50) sts along cuff row-end edge.

Row 1 (WS) P2, *K2, P2, rep from * to end.

Row 2 K2, *P2, K2, rep from * to end.

These 2 rows form rib.

Bind off in rib (on **WS**).

Sew side, sleeve, and cuff seams.

LOWER SECTION (worked downward)

With RS facing, using size 8 (5mm) needles and yarn **double**, beg and ending at front opening edges, pick up and knit 32 (34: 36) sts from bound-off edge of left front, 62 (66: 70) sts from cast-on edge of back, then 32 (34: 36) sts from bound-off edge of right front. 126 (134: 142) sts.

Beg with row 2, cont in patt as given for bodice and sleeves as follows:

Work 1 row, ending with RS facing for next row.

Change to size 10½ (7mm) needles.

Cont in patt until work meas 8¼ (9¾: 11) in [21 (25: 28) cm] from pick-up row, ending with RS facing for next row.

Beg with row 2, work in rib as given for cuffs for 2 rows, ending with RS facing for next row.

Bind off in rib.

FINISHING

Press carefully on WS, using a warm iron over a damp cloth.

Neckband

With RS facing, using size 8 (5mm) needles and yarn **double**, beg and ending at front opening edges, pick up and knit 62 (66: 70) sts evenly all around neck edge.

Beg with row 1, work in rib as given for cuffs for 2 rows, ending with **WS** facing for next row.

Bind off in rib (on **WS**).

Button border

With RS facing, using size 8 (5mm) needles and yarn **double**, pick up and knit 62 (74: 82) sts evenly down left front opening edge, from top of neckband to bound-off edge.

Beg with row 1, work in rib as given for cuffs for 2 rows, ending with **WS** facing for next row.

Bind off in rib (on **WS**).

Buttonhole border

With RS facing, using size 8 (5mm) needles and yarn **double**, pick up and knit 62 (74: 82) sts evenly up right front opening edge, from bound-off edge to top of neckband.

Beg with row 1, work in rib as given for cuffs as follows:

Next row (WS) Rib 2, *work 2 tog, yo (to make a buttonhole), rib 8 (9: 10), rep from * once more, work 2 tog, yo (to make 3rd buttonhole), rib to end.

Work in rib for 1 row, ending with **WS** facing for next row. Bind off in rib (on **WS**).

Sew on buttons.

Using size E/4 (3.50mm) crochet hook and yarn **single**, make five short chain belt loops. Sew to fronts, sides, and center back at lower edge of bodice. Thread ribbon through belt loops.

SLUMBER SLIPPERS

These lovely little slippers are perfect for padding around before bed. You will probably not want to take them off!

YARN

To fit		2-3 yrs	3-4 yrs	4-5 yrs
Length of foot		5¼in	6in	7in
		13.5cm	15.5cm	17.5cm

Rowan RYC Cashsoft Baby DK and Cashsoft DK

A	Baby DK Pale green (804)	1	1	1 x 50g/1¾oz
B	DK Lime green (509)	1	1	1 x 50g/1¾oz
C	DK Brown (517)	1	1	1 x 50g/1¾oz
D	DK Pale blue (503)	1	1	1 x 50g/1¾oz

NEEDLES

1 pair of size 6 (4mm) needles.

GAUGE

22 sts and 30 rows = 4in [10cm] square measured over pattern using size 6 (4mm) needles.

SLIPPERS (make 2)

Using size 6 (4mm) needles and yarn B, cast on 35 (39: 43) sts.
Break off yarn B and join in yarn A.
Row 1 (RS) K1, *P1, K1, rep from * to end.
Row 2 *P1, K1, rep from * to last st, inc in last st.
36 (40: 44) sts.
Cont in patt as follows:
Rows 1 and 2 Using yarn A, purl.
Row 3 (RS) Using yarn B, purl.
Row 4 Using yarn B, knit.
Rows 5 and 6 Using yarn A, purl.
Row 7 Using yarn C, purl.
Row 8 Using yarn C, knit.
Rows 9 and 10 Using yarn A, purl.
Row 11 Using yarn D, purl.
Row 12 Using yarn D, knit.
These 12 rows form patt.

Work 4 rows more in patt, ending with RS facing for next row.

Shape top of foot

Break off yarn and slip first 13 (14: 15) and last 13 (14: 15) sts onto holders.

Rejoin appropriate yarn to center 10 (12: 14) sts with RS facing and work 32 (38: 44) rows more in patt as set.

Break off contrasts and cont using yarn A only.

Next row (RS) (K2tog) 5 (6: 7) times. 5 (6: 7) sts.

Next row (K2tog) 1 (3: 2) times, (K3tog) 1 (0: 1) times. 2 (3: 3) sts.

Next row (K2tog) 1 (0: 0) times, (K3tog) 0 (1: 1) times and fasten off.

Place markers along row-end edge of this section 1½ (1¾: 2) in [4 (4.5: 5) cm] down from fasten-off point.

Shape first side

Return to sts left on holder and rejoin yarn A at end of last **complete** row worked.

With RS facing, K 13 (14: 15) sts left on holder, then pick up and knit 12 (14: 16) sts along side of top of foot to marker. 25 (28: 31) sts.

Work in g st for 11 (13: 15) rows, ending with RS facing for next row.

Next row (RS) K1, K2tog, K to end.

Next row K to last 3 sts, K2tog, K1.

Rep last 2 rows once more.

Bind off rem 21 (24: 27) sts.

Shape second side

With RS facing and yarn A, starting at marker along other side of top of foot, pick up and knit 12 (14: 16) sts along side of top of foot to sts left on holder, then K 13 (14: 15) sts left on holder. 25 (28: 31) sts.

Work in g st for 11 (13: 15) rows, ending with RS facing for next row.

Next row (RS) K to last 3 sts, K2tog, K1.

Next row K1, K2tog, K to end.

Rep last 2 rows once more.

Bind off rem 21 (24: 27) sts.

FINISHING

Do **not** press.

Sew toe seam, matching fasten-off point of top of foot to bound-off edges of side sections. Sew sole and heel seam.

SLUMBER HOT WATER BOTTLE COVER

So soft and comforting, this super hot water bottle cover is an ideal companion for slumbering—for everyone!

BEFORE YOU BEGIN

YARN

Size of cover   8½ x 15½in [22 x 39cm]

Rowan RYC Cashsoft Baby DK and Cashsoft DK

A Baby DK Pale green (804)   1 x 50g/1¾oz
B DK Lime green (509)   1 x 50g/1¾oz
C DK Brown (517)   1 x 50g/1¾oz
D DK Pale blue (503)   1 x 50g/1¾oz

NEEDLES

1 pair each of size 3 (3.25mm) and size 6 (4mm) needles.

BUTTONS

3

GAUGE

22 sts and 30 rows = 4in [10cm] square measured over pattern using size 6 (4mm) needles.

GETTING STARTED

LOWER BACK

Using size 6 (4mm) needles and yarn A, cast on 27 sts.

Joining in colors as required, cont in patt as follows:

Row 1 (RS) Using yarn A, purl.
Row 2 Using yarn A, cast on and P 6 sts, P to end.
Row 3 Using yarn B, cast on and P 6 sts, P to end. 39 sts.
Row 4 Using yarn B, inc in first st, K to last st, inc in last st.
Row 5 Using yarn A, inc in first st, P to last st, inc in last st.
Row 6 Rep row 5.
Row 7 Using yarn C, inc in first st, P to last st, inc in last st.
Row 8 Using yarn C, knit.
Row 9 Rep row 5. 49 sts.

Row 10 Rep row 1.
Row 11 Using yarn D, purl.
Row 12 Using yarn D, knit.
These 12 rows form patt and shape lower edge.**
Cont in patt for 40 rows more, ending after patt row 4 and with RS facing for next row.
Break off contrasts and cont using yarn A only.
Change to size 3 (3.25mm) needles.
Next row (RS) K1, *P1, K1, rep from * to end.
Next row P1, *K1, P1, rep from * to end.
These 2 rows form rib.
Work 4 rows more in rib, ending with RS facing for next row.
Next row (RS) Rib 9, (bind off 3 sts, rib until there are 11 sts on right needle after bind-off) twice, bind off 3 sts, rib to end.
Next row Rib to end, casting on 3 sts over those bound off on previous row.
Work 6 rows more in rib, ending with RS facing for next row.
Bind off in rib.

FRONT

Work as given for lower back to **.
Cont in patt for 62 rows more, ending after patt row 2 and with RS facing for next row.

Shape top

Keeping patt correct, dec 1 st at each end of next 4 rows. 41 sts.
Bind off 3 sts at beg of next 2 rows. 35 sts.
Dec 1 st at each end of next 3 rows, then on foll alt row, ending after patt row 1 and with **WS** facing for next row. 27 sts.
Break off contrasts and cont using yarn A only.
Change to size 3 (3.25mm) needles.
Beg with row 2, work in rib as given for lower back for 8in [20cm], ending with RS facing for next row.

Change to size 6 (4mm) needles.
Joining in colors as required, cont in patt as follows:

Row 1 (RS) Using yarn A, purl.

Row 2 Rep row 1.

Row 3 Using yarn D, inc in first st, P to last st, inc in last st.

Row 4 Using yarn D, inc in first st, K to last st, inc in last st.

Rows 5 and 6 Using yarn A, inc in first st, P to last st, inc in last st.

Row 7 Using yarn C, cast on and P 3 sts, P to end.

Row 8 Using yarn C, cast on and K 3 sts, K to end. 41 sts.

Rows 9 and 10 Rep rows 5 and 6.

Row 11 Using yarn B, inc in first st, P to last st, inc in last st.

Row 12 Using yarn B, inc in first st, K to last st, inc in last st. 49 sts.

These 12 rows form patt and shape top of back section.

Cont in patt as now set for 8 rows more, ending after patt row 8 and with RS facing for next row.

Break off contrasts and cont using yarn A only.

Change to size 3 (3.25mm) needles.

Work in rib as given for lower back for 14 rows, ending with RS facing for next row.

Bind off in rib.

FINISHING

Press pieces carefully on WS, using a warm iron over a damp cloth.

Overlap last 14 rows of front over last 14 rows of back and sew tog along side edges. Fold in half across center of narrow ribbed section, matching cast-on edges, and sew front to back along all edges. Sew on buttons.

SWEET DREAMS BLANKET

Delightfully soft and warm, this blanket with its large, dreamy flowers will look lovely on any little girl's bed. Sweet dreams!

YARN

Size of blanket   39½ x 41in [100 x 104cm]

Rowan RYC Cashsoft DK
Pale mauve (501)   13 x 50g/1¾oz

NEEDLES

1 pair each of long size 5 (3.75mm) and size 6 (4mm) needles **or** size 5 (3.75mm) and size 6 (4mm) circular needles.

GAUGE

22 sts and 30 rows = 4in [10cm] square measured over St st using size 6 (4mm) needles.

SPECIAL ABBREVIATION

MB = make bobble as follows: K into front, back, and front again of next st, (turn and K3) 4 times, slip 2nd and 3rd sts on right needle over first st and off right needle—bobble completed.

Push bobbles made on **WS** rows to **RS**.

BLANKET

Using size 5 (3.75mm) needles, cast on 245 sts. Work in g st for 32 rows, ending with RS facing for next row.
Change to size 6 (4mm) needles.

Place chart

Row 1 (RS) K17, work next 211 sts as row 1 of chart on page 62 (note that center 83 sts are repeated), K17.
Row 2 K17, work next 211 sts as row 2 of chart, K17.
These 2 rows set the sts—center 211 sts foll chart with 17 sts in g st at each side.
Cont as set until chart row 162 has been completed.
Now work chart rows 1 to 140 again, ending with RS facing for next row.
Change to size 5 (3.75mm) needles.
Work in g st for 33 rows, ending with **WS** facing for next row.
Bind off knitwise (on **WS**).

FINISHING

Press carefully on WS, using a warm iron over a damp cloth and being careful not to crush bobbles.

repeat these 83 sts twice

KEY

▚ knit on RS, purl on WS

▨ purl on RS, knit on WS

⬤ make bobble

SNUG CARDIGAN

Boys and girls will love this roomy, snug cardigan. The pockets are very useful for keeping bedtime snacks in!

BEFORE YOU BEGIN

YARN

Sizes	2-3 yrs	3-4 yrs	4-5 yrs
To fit chest	22in	24in	26in
	56cm	61cm	66cm
Actual size	30¼in	33in	35in
	77cm	84cm	89cm
Back length	15¼in	17¼in	19in
	39cm	44cm	48cm
Underarm seam	7½in	9in	10½in
	19cm	23cm	27cm

Rowan RYC Cashsoft Baby DK			
Pale green (804)	7	8	9 x 50g/1¾oz

NEEDLES & HOOK

1 pair each of size 3 (3.25mm) and size 6 (4mm) needles.
Cable needle.
Size E/4 (3.50mm) crochet hook.

BUTTON

1

GAUGE

30½ sts and 30 rows = 4in [10cm] square measured over cable patt using size 6 (4mm) needles.

SPECIAL ABBREVIATIONS

C4B = slip next 2 sts onto cable needle and leave at back of work, K2, then K2 from cable needle. **C4F** = slip next 2 sts onto cable needle and leave at front of work, K2, then K2 from cable needle. **C6B** = slip next 3 sts onto cable needle and leave at back of work, K3, then K3 from cable needle.

GETTING STARTED

BACK

Using size 3 (3.25mm) needles, cast on 85 (93: 99) sts.

Work in g st for 9 rows, ending with **WS** facing for next row.

Row 10 (WS) K0 (2: 3), (M1, K2) 0 (1: 2) times, *K2, (K1, M1) 3 times, K4, (M1, K2) twice, rep from * to last 7 (11: 14) sts, K2, (K1, M1) 3 times, K2, (K2, M1) 0 (1: 2) times, K0 (2: 3). 118 (128: 136) sts.
Change to size 6 (4mm) needles.
Cont in cable patt as follows:

Row 1 (RS) (P1, C4B) 0 (0: 1) times, K0 (1: 0), (C4F) 0 (1: 1) times, *P2, C6B, P2, C4B, C4F, rep from * to last 10 (15: 19) sts, P2, C6B, P2, (C4B) 0 (1: 1) times, K0 (1: 0), (C4F, P1) 0 (0: 1) times.

Row 2 and every foll alt row K0 (0: 1), P0 (5: 8), *K2, P6, K2, P8, rep from * to last 10 (15: 19) sts, K2, P6, K2, P0 (5: 8), K0 (0: 1).

Row 3 P0 (0: 1), K0 (5: 8), *P2, K6, P2, K8, rep from * to last 10 (15: 19) sts, P2, K6, P2, K0 (5: 8), P0 (0: 1).

Row 5 (P1, C4F) 0 (0: 1) times, K0 (1: 0), (C4B) 0 (1: 1) times, *P2, C6B, P2, C4F, C4B, rep from * to last 10 (15: 19) sts, P2, C6B, P2, (C4F) 0 (1: 1) times, K0 (1: 0), (C4B, P1) 0 (0: 1) times.

Row 7 Rep row 3.
Row 8 Rep row 2.
These 8 rows form cable patt.
Cont in patt until back meas 9½ (11: 12¼) in [24 (28: 31) cm], ending with RS facing for next row.

Shape armholes

Keeping patt correct, bind off 9 (10: 11) sts at beg of next 2 rows. 100 (108: 114) sts.
Dec 1 st at each end of next 5 rows, then on foll 2 (3: 3) alt rows, then on every foll 4th row until 82 (88: 94) sts rem.
Work even until armhole meas 6 (6¼: 6½) in [15 (16: 17) cm], ending with RS facing for next row.

Shape shoulders and back neck

Bind off 7 (8: 8) sts at beg of next 2 rows. 68 (72: 78) sts.

Next row (RS) Bind off 7 (8: 8) sts, patt until there are 13 (12: 13) sts on right needle and turn, leaving rem sts on a holder.

Work each side of neck separately.

Bind off 5 sts at beg of next row.

Bind off rem 8 (7: 8) sts.

With RS facing, rejoin yarn to rem sts, bind off center 28 (32: 36) sts, patt to end.

Complete to match first side, reversing shapings.

POCKET LININGS (make 2)

Using size 6 (4mm) needles, cast on 28 sts.

Work in cable patt as follows:

Row 1 (RS) P2, C6B, P2, C4B, C4F, P2, C6B, P2.

Row 2 and every foll alt row K2, P6, K2, P8, K2, P6, K2.

Row 3 P2, K6, P2, K8, P2, K6, P2.

Row 5 P2, C6B, P2, C4F, C4B, P2, C6B, P2.

Row 7 Rep row 3.

Row 8 Rep row 2.

These 8 rows form cable patt.

Work 14 rows more in patt, ending with RS facing for next row.

Break off yarn and leave sts on a holder.

LEFT FRONT

Using size 3 (3.25mm) needles, cast on 46 (50: 53) sts.

Work in g st for 9 rows, ending with **WS** facing for next row.

Row 10 (WS) *K2, (K1, M1) 3 times, K4, (M1, K2) twice, rep from * to last 7 (11: 14) sts, K2, (K1, M1) 3 times, K2, (K2, M1) 0 (1: 2) times, K0 (2: 3). 64 (69: 73) sts.

Change to size 6 (4mm) needles.

Work in cable patt as follows:

Row 1 (RS) (P1, C4B) 0 (0: 1) times, K0 (1: 0), (C4F) 0 (1: 1) times, *P2, C6B, P2, C4B, C4F, rep from * to last 10 sts, P2, C6B, P2.

Row 2 and every foll alt row *K2, P6, K2, P8, rep from * to last 10 (15: 19) sts, K2, P6, K2, P0 (5: 8), K0 (0: 1).

Row 3 P0 (0: 1), K0 (5: 8), *P2, K6, P2, K8, rep from * to last 10 sts, P2, K6, P2.

Row 5 (P1, C4F) 0 (0: 1) times, K0 (1: 0), (C4B) 0 (1: 1) times, *P2, C6B, P2, C4F, C4B, rep from * to last 10 sts, P2, C6B, P2.

Row 7 Rep row 3.

Row 8 Rep row 2.

These 8 rows form cable patt.

Work 14 rows more in patt, ending with RS facing for next row.

Place pocket

Next row (RS) Patt 18 (23: 27) sts, slip next 28 sts onto a holder and, in their place, patt across 28 sts of first pocket lining, patt to end.

Cont in patt until 6 rows less have been worked than on back to beg of armhole shaping, ending with RS facing for next row.

Shape front slope

Keeping patt correct, dec 1 st at end of next row and at same edge on foll 2 (4: 4) rows, then on foll 1 (0: 0) alt rows. 60 (64: 68) sts.

Work 1 row, ending with RS facing for next row.

Shape armhole

Keeping patt correct, bind off 9 (10: 11) sts at beg and dec 1 st at end of next row. 50 (53: 56) sts.

Work 1 row.

Dec 1 st at armhole edge of next 5 rows, then on foll 2 (3: 3) alt rows, then on 2 foll 4th rows *and at same time* dec 1 st at front slope edge on next and every foll alt row. 32 (33: 36) sts.

Dec 1 st at front slope edge only on 2nd and every foll alt row until 22 (23: 24) sts rem.

Work even until left front matches back to beg of shoulder shaping, ending with RS facing for next row.

Shape shoulder

Bind off 7 (8: 8) sts at beg of next and foll alt row.

Work 1 row. Bind off rem 8 (7: 8) sts.

RIGHT FRONT

Using size 3 (3.25mm) needles, cast on 46 (50: 53) sts.

Work in g st for 9 rows, ending with **WS** facing for next row.

Row 10 (WS) K0 (2: 3), (M1, K2) 0 (1: 2) times, *K2, (K1, M1) 3 times, K4, (M1, K2) twice, rep from * to last 7 sts, K2, (K1, M1) 3 times, K2. 64 (69: 73) sts.

Change to size 6 (4mm) needles.

Work in cable patt as follows:

Row 1 (RS) *P2, C6B, P2, C4B, C4F, rep from * to

last 10 (15: 19) sts, P2, C6B, P2, (C4B) 0 (1: 1) times, K0 (1: 0), (C4F, P1) 0 (0: 1) times.

Row 2 and every foll alt row K0 (0: 1), P0 (5: 8), *K2, P6, K2, P8, rep from * to last 10 sts, K2, P6, K2.

Row 3 *P2, K6, P2, K8, rep from * to last 10 (15: 19) sts, P2, K6, P2, K0 (5: 8), P0 (0: 1).

Row 5 *P2, C6B, P2, C4F, C4B, rep from * to last 10 (15: 19) sts, P2, C6B, P2, (C4F) 0 (1: 1) times, K0 (1: 0), (C4B, P1) 0 (0: 1) times.

Row 7 Rep row 3.

Row 8 Rep row 2.

These 8 rows form cable patt.

Work 14 rows more in patt, ending with RS facing for next row.

Place pocket

Next row (RS) Patt 18 sts, slip next 28 sts onto a holder and, in their place, patt across 28 sts of second pocket lining, patt to end.

Complete to match left front, reversing shapings.

SLEEVES

Using size 3 (3.25mm) needles, cast on 44 (46: 48) sts.

Work in g st for 9 rows, ending with **WS** facing for next row.

Row 10 (WS) K1 (2: 3), * (K1, M1) 3 times, K2, (K2, M1) twice, K4, rep from * to last 4 (5: 6) sts, (K1, M1) 3 times, K1 (2: 3). 62 (64: 66) sts.

Change to size 6 (4mm) needles.

Cont in cable patt as follows:

Row 1 (RS) K0 (0: 1), P1 (2: 2), *C6B, P2, C4B, C4F, P2, rep from * to last 7 (8: 9) sts, C6B, P1 (2: 2), K0 (0: 1).

Row 2 P0 (0: 1), K1 (2: 2), *P6, K2, P8, K2, rep from * to last 7 (8: 9) sts, P6, K1 (2: 2), P0 (0: 1).

These 2 rows set position of cable patt as given for back.

Cont in cable patt, shaping sides by inc 1 st at each end of next (3rd: 3rd) and every foll alt (4th: 4th) row until there are 66 (84: 80) sts, then on every foll 4th (6th: 6th) row until there are 84 (88: 92) sts, taking inc sts into patt.

Work even until sleeve meas 7½ (9: 10½) in [19 (23: 27) cm], ending with RS facing for next row.

Shape sleeve cap

Keeping patt correct, bind off 9 (10: 11) sts at

beg of next 2 rows. 66 (68: 70) sts.

Dec 1 st at each end of every row until 26 sts rem, ending with RS (WS: RS) facing for next row.

Bind off in patt.

FINISHING

Press pieces very lightly on WS, using a warm iron over a damp cloth.

Pocket tops (both alike)

Slip 28 sts from pocket holder onto size 3 (3.25mm) needles and rejoin yarn with RS facing.

Work in g st for 9 rows, ending with **WS** facing for next row.

Bind off knitwise (on **WS**).

Sew pocket linings neatly in place on WS, then sew down ends of pocket tops.

Sew shoulder seams using backstitch, or mattress stitch if preferred. Sew side seams. Sew sleeve seams. Sew in sleeves.

Crochet edging

With RS facing and using size E/4 (3.50mm) crochet hook, attach yarn at base of right front opening edge, ch1 (does *not* count as st), work 1 row of sc evenly up right front opening and around neck edge, then work chains at beg of left front neck shaping to make a button loop big enough to fit button. Cont sc edging down left front, ending at base. Fasten off. Sew on button.

SNUG SOCKS

The softest, warmest, and most roomy socks, these will keep anyone's toes cozy in and out of bed.

YARN

To fit	2-3 yrs	3-4 yrs	4-5 yrs
Length of foot	5¼in	5¾in	6in
	13.5cm	14.5cm	15.5cm
Rowan RYC Cashsoft Baby DK			
Pale green (804)	2	2	2 x 50g/1¾oz

NEEDLES

1 pair each of size 3 (3.25mm) and size 5 (3.75mm) needles.
Cable needle.

GAUGE

Based on a St st gauge of 22 sts and 30 rows = 4in [10cm] square using size 6 (4mm) needles.

SPECIAL ABBREVIATIONS

C4B = slip next 2 sts onto cable needle and leave at back of work, K2, then K2 from cable needle; **C4F** = slip next 2 sts onto cable needle and leave at front of work, K2, then K2 from cable needle.

GETTING STARTED

SOCKS (make 2)

Using size 3 (3.25mm) needles, cast on 36 sts.
Work in g st for 3 rows, ending with **WS** facing for next row.
Row 4 (WS) (K2, inc once in each of next 2 sts, K2, inc once in each of next 4 sts) 3 times, K2, inc once in each of next 2 sts, K2. 56 sts.
Change to size 5 (3.75mm) needles.
Cont in cable patt as follows:
Row 1 (RS) *(P2, C4B) twice, C4F, rep from * twice more, P2, C4B, P2.
Row 2 and every foll alt row (K2, P4, K2, P8) 3 times, K2, P4, K2.
Row 3 (P2, K4, P2, K8) 3 times, P2, K4, P2.
Row 5 (P2, C4B, P2, C4F, C4B) 3 times, P2, C4B, P2.
Row 7 Rep row 3.
Row 8 Rep row 2.
These 8 rows form cable patt.
Cont in cable patt until sock meas 5in [13cm], ending with RS facing for next row.

Shape top of foot

Break off yarn.
Slip first 14 sts and last 14 sts onto holders.
With RS facing and using size 5 (3.75mm) needles, rejoin yarn to center 28 sts and cont as follows:
Next row (RS) K1, sl 1, K1, psso, patt to last 3 sts, K2tog, K1. 26 sts.
Next row P2, patt to last 2 sts, P2.
Next row K2, patt to last 2 sts, K2.
Last 2 rows set the sts.
Cont as set for 22 (24: 28) rows more, ending with **WS** facing for next row.
Next row (WS) P2, K1, (P2tog) twice, K2, (P2tog) 4 times, K2, (P2tog) twice, K1, P2. 18 sts.

Shape toe

Next row (RS) K2, sl 1, K1, psso, K to last 4 sts, K2tog, K2.
Next row P2, P2tog, P to last 4 sts, P2tog tbl, P2.
Rep last 2 rows twice more. 6 sts.

Next row (RS) (K2tog) 3 times.
Bind off rem 3 sts (on **WS**).

Shape heel

Slip the two sets of 14 sts from holders onto a size 5 (3.75mm) needle, with row-end edges meeting at center. Rejoin yarn to these 28 sts with RS facing and cont as follows:
Next row (RS) (K2tog) 3 times, K2, (K2tog) twice, K4, (K2tog) twice, K2, (K2tog) 3 times. 18 sts.
Beg with a P row, work 9 rows in St st, ending with RS facing for next row.

Turn heel

Row 1 (RS) K9, K2tog tbl, K1 and turn.
Row 2 Sl 1, P1, P2tog, P1 and turn.
Row 3 Sl 1, K2, K2tog tbl, K1 and turn.
Row 4 Sl 1, P3, P2tog, P1 and turn.

Row 5 Sl 1, K4, K2tog tbl, K1 and turn.
Row 6 Sl 1, P5, P2tog, P1 and turn.
Row 7 Sl 1, K6, K2tog tbl, K1 and turn.
Row 8 Sl 1, P7, P2tog, P1. 10 sts.
Break off yarn.
With RS facing, and using size 5 (3.75mm) needles, pick up and knit 10 sts along row-end edge of first side of heel, K 10 heel sts, then pick up and knit 10 sts along other side of heel. 30 sts.
Next row (WS) Purl.
Next row K2, sl 1, K1, psso, K to last 4 sts, K2tog, K2.
Next row Purl.
Rep last 2 rows 5 times more. 18 sts.
Work 12 (14: 18) rows more, ending with RS facing for next row.
Complete as given for top of foot from beg of toe shaping.

FINISHING

Press pieces very lightly on WS, using a warm iron over a damp cloth.

Sew heel seam. Sew foot and toe seams.

OTTO OWL TOY

Otto Owl is a great thinker. I believe he is thinking now. He gets his best thoughts, however, sitting in a tree with friends.

YARN

Size of toy   8½ x 9½ in [21 x 24cm]

Rowan RYC Cashsoft DK

A Brown (517)   2 x 50g/1¾oz
B Beige (515)   1 x 50g/1¾oz
C Lime green (509)   1 x 50g/1¾oz
D Pale blue (503)   1 x 50g/1¾oz

Note: For the alternative scarf colors, use Cashsoft DK Pale mauve (501) or Pale blue (503).

NEEDLES

1 pair of size 6 (4mm) needles.

EXTRAS

Washable toy filling.

GAUGE

22 sts and 30 rows = 4in [10cm] square measured over St st using size 6 (4mm) needles.

SPECIAL ABBREVIATION

MB = make beak over 2 sts as follows: inc once in each of next 2 sts, (turn and P4, turn and K4) 4 times, turn and P4, turn and (K2tog) twice.

GETTING STARTED

FRONT Ⓐ

Using size 6 (4mm) needles and yarn A, cast on 30 sts.

Beg with a P row, work in striped rev St st as follows:

Row 1 Using yarn A, purl.
Row 2 Using yarn A, inc in first st, K to last st, inc in last st.
Join in yarn B.
Row 3 Using yarn B, inc in first st, P to last st, inc in last st.
Row 4 Using yarn B, inc in first st, K to last st, inc in last st. 36 sts.
Last 4 rows form striped rev St st and beg shaping.
Cont in striped rev St st, inc 1 st at each end of next 3 rows, then on foll alt row, then on foll 4th row. 46 sts.
Work 29 rows, ending after 2 rows using yarn A and with RS facing for next row.
Break off yarn B and cont using yarn A only.
Beg with a K row, work in St st, dec 1 st at each end of next and foll 6th row. 42 sts.
Work 1 row, ending with RS facing for next row.**
Using the *intarsia* technique, work foll chart, which is worked entirely in St st beg with a K row (chart row 1), as follows:
Keeping chart patt correct, dec 1 st at each end of 8th and foll 6th row, then on foll alt row, ending after chart row 16 has been completed and with RS facing for next row. 36 sts.
Cont in St st, beg with a K row, using yarn A only.

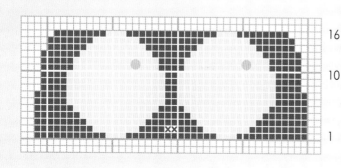

16

10

1

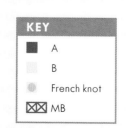

KEY	
◼	A
▫	B
⬤	French knot
⊠⊠	MB

Dec 1 st at each end of next 5 rows, ending with **WS** facing for next row.
Bind off rem 26 sts purlwise (on **WS**).

BACK **B**

Work as given for front to **.
Dec 1 st at each end of 8th and foll 6th row, then on foll alt row, then on foll 5 rows, ending with **WS** facing for next row.
Bind off rem 26 sts purlwise (on **WS**).

BASE **C**

Using size 6 (4mm) needles and yarn A, cast on 3 sts.
Beg with a K row, work in St st as follows:
Work 1 row.
Inc 1 st at each end of next 6 rows. 15 sts.
Work 27 rows, ending with RS facing for next row.
Dec 1 st at each end of next 6 rows, ending with RS facing for next row.
Bind off rem 3 sts.

WINGS **D** (make 4)

Using size 6 (4mm) needles and yarn A, cast on 21 sts.
Rows 1 and 2 Knit.
Row 3 K3 and turn.
Row 4 and every foll alt row Knit.

Row 5 K6 and turn.
Row 7 K9 and turn.
Row 9 K12 and turn.
Row 11 K15 and turn.
Row 12 Knit.
Rep rows 1 to 12 three times more.
Bind off.

TAIL **E** (make 2)

Using size 6 (4mm) needles and yarn A, cast on 15 sts.
Rows 1 and 2 Knit.
Row 3 K3 and turn.
Row 4 and every foll alt row Knit.
Row 5 K6 and turn.
Row 7 K9 and turn.
Row 10 Knit.
Rep rows 1 to 10 three times more.
Bind off.

EARS **F** (make 4)

Using size 6 (4mm) needles and yarn A, cast on 6 sts.
Work in g st for 15 rows, ending with **WS** facing for next row.
Row 16 (WS) K1, K2tog, sl 1, K1, psso, K1. 4 sts.
Row 17 (K2tog) twice.
Row 18 K2tog and fasten off.

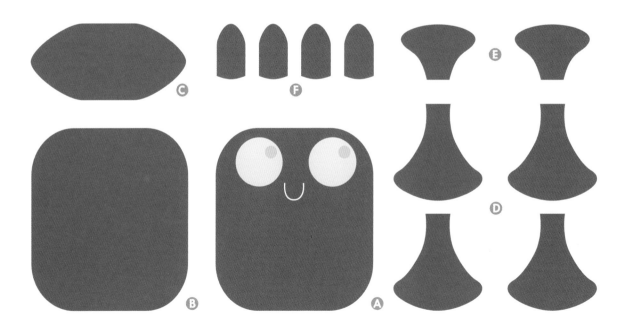

76

SCARF

Using size 6 (4mm) needles and yarn C, cast on
11 sts.
Work in g st for 27in [68cm]. Bind off.

FINISHING

Press pieces carefully on WS, using a warm iron
over a damp cloth.

Sew pairs of ear pieces together, leaving cast-
on edges open. Sew front to back, leaving cast-
on edges open and enclosing ears in seam as in
photograph. Sew pairs of tail pieces together,
leaving shorter row-end edges open. Sew base

to cast-on edges of back and front, leaving an
opening to insert toy filling and enclosing tail in
seam at center back. Insert toy filling then sew
opening closed. Sew tail to back about 1¼in
[3cm] above base seam. Sew pairs of wing
pieces together, leaving shorter row-end edges
open. Sew shorter row-end edges to sides of
owl, level with last row of rev St st. Sew
together row-end edges of scarf. Cut 3in [8cm]
lengths of yarn D (or C) and knot these lengths
through ends of scarf to form fringe. Using chart
as a guide and yarn D, embroider French knots
onto eyes. Sew together sides of beak.

ROOST BLANKET

Wrap up in this gorgeous embroidered blanket for a bedtime story. The sleepy birds will help you nod off.

YARN

Size of blanket   41½ x 43½in [106 x 111cm]

Rowan RYC Cashsoft DK and Cashsoft Baby DK

A DK Gray (518)	11 x 50g/1¾oz
B DK Lime green (509)	2 x 50g/1¾oz
C DK Pale blue (503)	2 x 50g/1¾oz
D DK Orange (510)	1 x 50g/1¾oz
E Baby DK Pale green (804)	2 x 50g/1¾oz

NEEDLES

1 pair of size 3 (3.25mm) needles.
1 pair of long size 6 (4mm) needles **or** size 6 (4mm) circular needle.

GAUGE

22 sts and 30 rows = 4in [10cm] square measured over St st using size 6 (4mm) needles.

MAIN SECTION

Using size 6 (4mm) needles and yarn A, cast on 218 sts.
Beg with a K row, work in St st for 8 rows, ending with RS facing for next row.
Joining in and breaking off colors as required, cont as follows:
**Row 1 (RS) Using yarn E, purl.
Row 2 Using yarn E, knit.
Rows 3 and 4 Using yarn A, purl.
Row 5 Using yarn C, purl.
Row 6 Using yarn C, knit.
Rows 7 and 8 Using yarn A, purl.
Row 9 Using yarn B, purl.
Row 10 Using yarn B, knit.
Rows 11 and 12 Using yarn A, purl.
Rows 13 to 24 Rep rows 1 to 12.
Rows 25 to 28 Rep rows 5 to 8.
Rows 29 to 32 Rep rows 1 to 4.

Rows 33 to 36 Rep rows 9 to 12.
Rows 37 to 40 Rep rows 5 to 8.
Rows 41 and 42 Rep rows 1 and 2.
These 42 rows complete textured patt band.***
Beg with a K row, work in St st using yarn A for 18 rows, ending with RS facing for next row.**
Using the *intarsia* technique, work 62 rows foll chart 1 (see pages 82 and 83), which is worked entirely in St st beg with a K row (chart row 1).
Beg with a K row, work in St st using yarn A for 18 rows, ending with RS facing for next row.
Rep from ** to ** once more.
Using the *intarsia* technique, work 62 rows foll chart 2, which is worked entirely in St st beg with a K row (chart row 1).
Beg with a K row, work in St st using yarn A for 18 rows, ending with RS facing for next row.
Rep from ** to *** once more.
Beg with a K row, work in St st using yarn A for 8 rows, ending with RS facing for next row.
Bind off.

FINISHING

Press blanket carefully using a warm iron over a damp cloth.

Embroidery

Using yarn B, work long stitches over wing sts as indicted on charts, securing them with short couching stitches worked on every other row.
Using charts as a guide and yarn D, embroider three short straight stitches over branch at base of each leg to form feet.
Using charts as a guide and yarn E, work cross-stitches along branches, placing one on every 3rd st. Using yarn E, embroider a French knot in center of each leaf.

Borders (make 4)

Using size 3 (3.25mm) needles and yarn A, cast on 3 sts.

Row 1 (RS) Inc in first st, P1, inc in last st.
Row 2 and every foll alt row Knit.
Row 3 Inc in first st, K1, P1, K1, inc in last st.
Row 5 Inc in first st, (P1, K1) twice, P1, inc in last st.
Row 7 Inc in first st, (K1, P1) 3 times, K1, inc in last st.
Row 9 Inc in first st, (P1, K1) 4 times, P1, inc in last st.

Row 11 Inc in first st, (K1, P1) 5 times, K1, inc in last st.
Row 13 Inc in first st, (P1, K1) 6 times, P1, inc in last st.
Row 15 Inc in first st, (K1, P1) 7 times, K1, inc in last st. 19 sts.
Cont in patt as follows:
Row 16 (WS) Knit.
Row 17 K1, *P1, K1, rep from * to end.
These 2 rows form patt.
Cont in patt until shorter edge, when slightly stretched, fits along one side of main section, ending with RS facing for next row.
　　Keeping patt correct, dec 1 st at each end of next and every foll alt row until 3 sts rem.
　　Work 1 row, ending with RS facing for next row.
Next row (RS) K3tog and fasten off.

Sew edges of borders to outer edges of main section. Sew mitered corner seams of borders, then fold borders in half to WS and slip stitch in place.

chart 1 (continued)

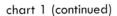

chart 2 (continued)

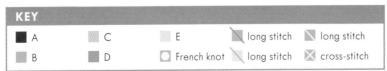

KEY				
■ A	▨ C	▧ E	◸ long stitch	◹ long stitch
▨ B	▨ D	○ French knot	◺ long stitch	⊠ cross-stitch

chart 1

chart 2

ROOST PJ CASE

Keep your pajamas and bed socks neat and tidy in this roomy PJ case. It's very stylish!

YARN

Size of case   11 x 7½in [28 x 19cm]

Rowan RYC Cashsoft DK and Cashsoft Baby DK

A DK Pale blue (503)   2 x 50g/1¾ oz
B Baby DK Pale green (804)   1 x 50g/1¾ oz
C DK Orange (510)   1 x 50g/1¾ oz
D DK Lime green (509)   1 x 50g/1¾ oz

NEEDLES & HOOK

1 pair of size 6 (4mm) needles.
Size E/4 (3.50mm) crochet hook.

GAUGE

22 sts and 30 rows = 4in [10cm] square measured over St st using size 6 (4mm) needles.

BACK

Using size 6 (4mm) needles and yarn A, cast on 22 sts.
Beg with a K row, work in St st as follows:
Work 1 row.
Cast on 5 sts at beg of next 2 rows, then 4 sts at beg of foll 2 rows. 40 sts.
Inc 1 st at each end of next 8 rows, then on foll alt row, then on every foll 3rd row until there are 62 sts, ending with **WS** facing for next row.**
Work 35 rows, ending with RS facing for next row.
Next row K2, *P2, K2, rep from * to end.
Next row P2, *K2, P2, rep from * to end.
Rep last 2 rows twice more.
Bind off in rib.

FRONT

Work as given for back to **.
Work 41 rows, ending with RS facing for next row.

Shape flap

Place markers at ends of last row.
Work 6 rows.
Next row (RS) K1, sl 1, K1, psso, K to last 3 sts, K2tog, K1.
Work 3 rows.
Rep last 4 rows 3 times more. 54 sts.
Next row (RS) K1, sl 1, K1, psso, K to last 3 sts, K2tog, K1.
Work 1 row.
Rep last 2 rows 13 times more. 26 sts.
Next row (RS) K1, sl 1, K1, psso, K to last 3 sts, K2tog, K1.
Next row P1, P2tog, P to last 3 sts, P2tog tbl, P1.
Rep last 2 rows 4 times more. 6 sts.
Next row (RS) K1, sl 1, K1, psso, K2tog, K1.
Next row P2tog, P2tog tbl.
Next row K2tog and fasten off.

WING (make 2)

Using size 6 (4mm) needles and yarn B, cast on 14 sts.
Beg with a K row, work in St st as follows:
Work 1 row.
Cast on 3 sts at beg of next 2 rows. 20 sts.
Inc 1 st at each end of next 5 rows, then on foll alt row, then on foll 4th row, ending with RS facing for next row. 34 sts.
Work 28 rows, ending with RS facing for next row. Bind off.

BEAK (make 2)

Using size 6 (4mm) needles and yarn B, cast on 21 sts.
Beg with a K row, work in St st as follows:
Work 3 rows, ending with **WS** facing for next row.

Dec 1 st at each end of next and every foll 3rd row until 13 sts rem, then on every foll alt row until 3 sts rem, ending with **WS** facing for next row.
Next row (WS) P3tog and fasten off.

TAIL (make 2)

Using size 6 (4mm) needles and yarn B, cast on 25 sts.
Beg with a K row, work in St st as follows:
Work 16 rows, ending with RS facing for next row.

Divide for tail feathers

Next row (RS) K5, K2tog and turn, leaving rem sts on a holder.

Work each feather separately.
Work 2 rows, ending with **WS** facing for next row.
Dec 1 st at beg of next row and at same edge on foll 3rd row, then on foll alt row, ending with **WS** facing for next row.
Bind off rem 3 sts purlwise.
With RS facing, rejoin yarn to rem sts and cont as follows:
Next row (RS) K2tog, K7, K2tog and turn, leaving rem sts on a holder.
Dec 1 st at each end of 3rd and foll 3rd row, then on foll alt row, ending with **WS** facing for next row.

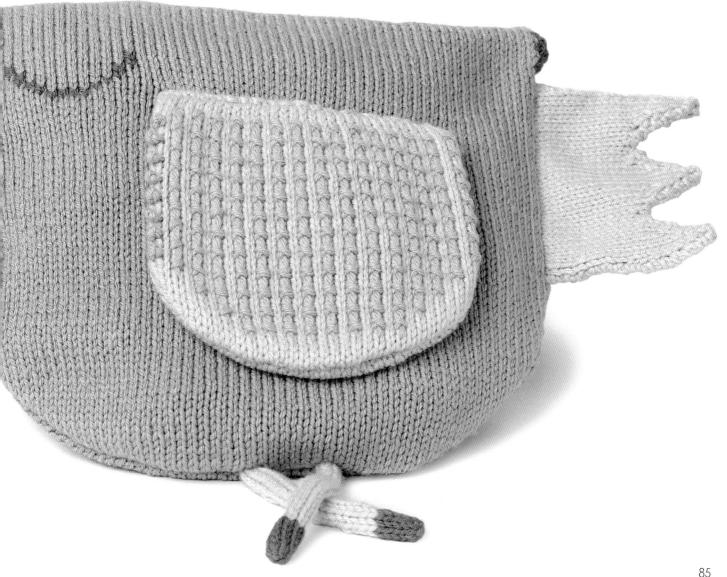

chart 1

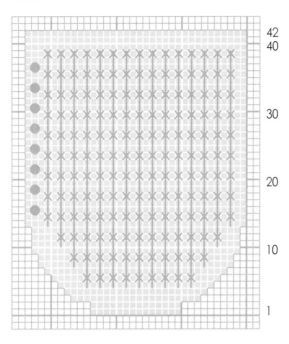

42
40

30

20

10

1

Bind off rem 3 sts purlwise.

With RS facing, rejoin yarn to rem sts and cont as follows:

Next row (RS) K2tog, K5.

Work 2 rows, ending with **WS** facing for next row.

Dec 1 st at end of next row and at same edge on foll 3rd row, then on foll alt row, ending with **WS** facing for next row.

Bind off rem 3 sts purlwise.

LEGS (make 2)

Using size 6 (4mm) needles and yarn C, cast on 6 sts.

Beg with a K row, work in St st as follows:

Work 4 rows, ending with RS facing for next row.

Break off yarn C and join in yarn B.

Cont in St st until leg meas 4in [10cm]. Bind off.

FINISHING

Press pieces carefully on WS, using a warm iron over a damp cloth.

Embroidery

Using yarn D, embroider decoration on one wing piece following chart 1. Work long straight stitches over wing sts as indicated on chart,

chart 2

7

1

KEY	
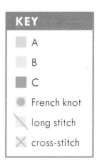	A
	B
	C
●	French knot
╲	long stitch
✕	cross-stitch

securing them with cross-stitches worked on every 3rd row. At front edge of wing, embroider a row of French knots.

Using yarn C, duplicate stitch eye on front following chart 2 and positioning chart 7 sts in from front edge and 11 rows below marked row.

With RS tog, sew tog wing pieces along row-end and cast-on edges. Turn RS out and sew bound-off edges closed. Using photograph as a guide, sew bound-off edges of wing to front, about 18 rows below marked row. With RS tog, sew tog beak pieces, leaving cast-on edges open. Turn RS out and sew cast-on edges closed. With WS tog, sew tog tail pieces. With WS tog, sew tog row-end and cast-on edges of legs.

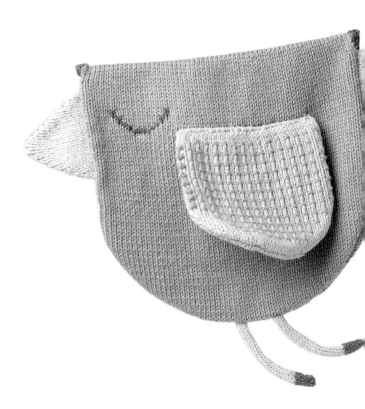

Using photograph as a guide and matching bound-off edge of back to markers on front, sew back to front, enclosing legs, tail, and beak in seam so that tail and beak are just below markers.

Crochet edging

With RS facing, using size E/4 (3.50mm) crochet hook and yarn C, attach yarn at top of seam above tail, ch1 (does *not* count as st), 1sc into place where yarn was attached, now work around outer edge of flap and across bound-off edge of back as follows: *ch1, 1sc into edge, rep from * to end, replacing sc at end of last rep with 1 slip st into first sc.

Next row (RS) Ch1 (does *not* count as st), 1sc into first ch sp, *ch1, skip 1sc, 1sc into next ch sp, rep from * to top of seam above beak.

Fasten off.

COZY TANK TOP

Cozy, cute, and very, very soft, this little tank top with its pretty pocket is perfect as an extra layer over pajamas.

YARN

Sizes	2-3 yrs	3-4 yrs	4-5 yrs
To fit chest	22in	24in	26in
	56cm	61cm	66cm
Actual size	25½in	27½in	29½in
	65cm	70cm	75cm
Back length	12½in	14½in	16in
	32cm	37cm	41cm

Rowan RYC Cashsoft DK and Cashsoft Baby DK			
A DK Brown (517)	1	1	2 x 50g/1¾oz
B Baby DK Pale green (804)	2	2	3 x 50g/1¾oz

NEEDLES & HOOK

1 pair each of size 5 (3.75mm) and size 6 (4mm) needles.
Size E/4 (3.50mm) crochet hook.

EXTRAS

12in [30cm] of narrow ribbon.

GAUGE

22 sts and 30 rows = 4in [10cm] square measured over main pattern using size 6 (4mm) needles.

GETTING STARTED

BACK

Using size 6 (4mm) needles and yarn A, cast on 83 (89: 95) sts.
Row 1 (RS) P2, *yo, K1, yo, P2, rep from * to end. 137 (147: 157) sts.
Row 2 K2, *P3, K2, rep from * to end.
Row 3 P2, *K3, P2, rep from * to end.
Row 4 K2, *P3tog, K2, rep from * to end. 83 (89: 95) sts.
Break off yarn A and join in yarn B.
Cont in main patt as follows:
Row 1 (RS) Knit.
Row 2 Purl.

Row 3 K1 (0: 3), *P1, K3, rep from * to last 2 (1: 0) sts, P1 (1: 0), K1 (0: 0).
Row 4 Purl.
Row 5 Knit.
Row 6 P3 (2: 1), *K1, P3, rep from * to last 0 (3: 2) sts, K0 (1: 1), P0 (2: 1).
These 6 rows form main patt.
Cont in main patt for 8 rows more, ending with RS facing for next row.**
Dec 1 st at each end of next and every foll 12th (14th: 16th) row until 77 (83: 89) sts rem.
***Work even until back meas 6½ (8¼ : 9½) in [17 (21: 24) cm], ending with RS facing for next row.
Break off yarn B and join in yarn A.
Change to size 5 (3.75mm) needles.
Next row (RS) K8, *K2tog, K10 (11: 12), rep from * 4 times more, K2tog, K to end. 71 (77: 83) sts.
Cont in yoke patt as follows:
Row 1 (WS) K0 (0: 1), P1 (0: 2), *K2, P2, rep from * to last 2 (1: 0) sts, K2 (1: 0).
Row 2 Rep row 1.
These 2 rows form yoke patt.
Cont in yoke patt until back meas 9 (10½: 11¾) in [23 (27: 30) cm], ending with RS facing for next row.

Shape armholes

Keeping patt correct, bind off 6 sts at beg of next 2 rows. 59 (65: 71) sts.
Dec 1 st at each end of next 3 rows, then on foll 1 (2: 3) alt rows. 51 (55: 59) sts.
Work even until armhole meas 2 (2¼: 2¾) in [5 (6: 7) cm], ending with RS facing for next row.

Shape neck

Next row (RS) Patt 20 (21: 22) sts and turn, leaving rem sts on a holder.
Work each side of neck separately.
Bind off 4 sts at beg of next row. 16 (17: 18) sts.

Dec 1 st at neck edge on next 5 rows, then on foll 2 alt rows. 9 (10: 11) sts.
Work even until armhole meas 3½ (4: 4¼) in [9 (10: 11) cm], ending with RS facing for next row.

Shape shoulder
Bind off 4 (5: 5) sts at beg of next row.
Work 1 row.
Bind off rem 5 (5: 6) sts.
With RS facing, rejoin yarn to rem sts, bind off center 11 (13: 15) sts, patt to end. 20 (21: 22) sts.
Complete to match first side, reversing shapings.

FRONT
Work as given for back to **.

Place pocket
Next row (RS) K2tog, patt 52 (55: 58) sts, slip next 15 sts onto a holder for pocket front, cast on 15 sts onto right needle, patt to last 2 sts, K2tog. 81 (87: 93) sts.
Dec 1 st at each end of 12th (14th: 16th) and foll 12th (14th: 16th) row. 77 (83: 89) sts.
Complete as given for back from ***.

FINISHING
Press pieces carefully on WS, using a warm iron over a damp cloth.

Pocket front
Slip 15 sts from pocket front holder onto size 6 (4mm) needles and rejoin yarn A with RS facing.
Row 1 (RS) Inc in first st, K2, (P1, K3) twice, P1, K2, inc in last st. 17 sts.
Row 2 Purl.
Row 3 Knit.
Row 4 P2, (K1, P3) 3 times, K1, P2.
Row 5 Knit.
Row 6 Purl.
These 6 rows form patt.
Work 8 rows more in patt, ending with RS facing for next row.
Row 15 (RS) P2, (yo, K1, yo, P2) 5 times. 27 sts.
Row 16 K2, (P3, K2) 5 times.
Row 17 P2, (K3, P2) 5 times.
Row 18 K2, (P3tog, K2) 5 times.
Bind off rem 17 sts.

Neatly sew pocket front in place. Sew both shoulder seams using backstitch, or mattress stitch if preferred. Sew side seams.

Crochet hem edging
With RS facing, using size E/4 (3.50mm) crochet hook and yarn B, attach yarn to cast-on edge at base of one side seam, ch1 (does **not** count as st), 1sc into edge, *ch1, 1sc into edge, rep from * to end, replacing sc at end of last rep with 1 slip st into first sc.
Fasten off.

Using yarn A, work crochet edging around neck and armhole edges in same way.

Using photograph as a guide, thread ribbon through row 15 of pocket front and tie in bow at center.

BELLA BUNNY

Bella Bunny is very balletic. She likes dancing, hopping about, and eating little cakes.

GETTING STARTED

BODY A (make 2)

Using size 2 (2.75mm) needles and yarn A, cast on 30 sts.
Beg with a K row, work in St st as follows:
Work 8 rows, ending with RS facing for next row.
Dec 1 st at each end of next and every foll 6th row to 16 sts, then on foll 5th row. 14 sts.
Work 1 row, ending with WS facing for next row.

Shape head

Inc 1 st at each end of next and foll 2 alt rows, then on foll 3rd row. 22 sts.
Work 7 rows, ending with RS facing for next row.
Dec 1 st at each end of next and foll 4 alt rows.
Work 1 row, ending with RS facing for next row.
Bind off rem 12 sts.

LEGS B (make 2)

Using size 2 (2.75mm) needles and yarn A, cast on 14 sts.

Beg with a K row, work in St st as follows:
Work 46 rows, ending with RS facing for next row.
**Next row (RS) K1, (sl 1, K1, psso) 6 times, K1. 8 sts.
Next row (P2tog) 4 times. 4 sts.
Next row (K2tog) twice. 2 sts.
Next row P2tog and fasten off.

ARMS C (make 2)

Using size 2 (2.75mm) needles and yarn A, cast on 14 sts.
Beg with a K row, work in St st as follows:
Work 26 rows, ending with RS facing for next row.
Complete as given for legs from **.

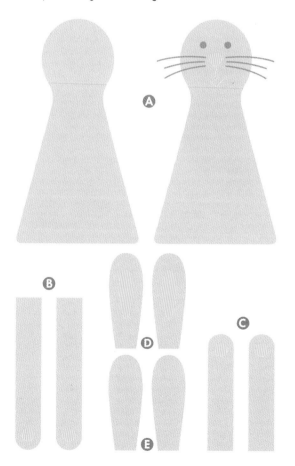

chart 1

attach ears here

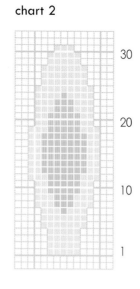

27

20

10

1

chart 2

30

20

10

1

INNER EARS Ⓓ (make 2)

Using size 2 (2.75mm) needles and yarn A, cast on 5 sts.

Using the *intarsia* technique, cont foll chart 2, which is worked entirely in St st beg with a K row (chart row 1), as follows:

Keeping chart patt correct, inc 1 st at each end of 5th and foll 3rd row, then on foll 4th row. 11 sts.

Work 7 rows, ending with **WS** facing for next row.

Dec 1 st at each end of next and foll 6th row, then on foll 3rd row, then on foll alt row, ending with **WS** facing for next row.
Bind off rem 3 sts purlwise (on **WS**).

OUTER EARS  (make 2)

Work as given for inner ears, but using yarn A throughout.

NOSE AND PADS (make 5)

Using size C/2 (2.50mm) crochet hook and yarn B, ch4 and join with a slip st to form a ring.
Round 1 (RS) Ch1 (does *not* count as st), (1sc into ring, ch1) 4 times, join with a slip st to first sc. Fasten off.

FINISHING

Press pieces carefully on WS, using a warm iron over a damp cloth.

Using photograph as a guide, sew pads to arms and legs. Using chart 1 as a guide, sew nose to face. Using yarn B, embroider mouth below nose by working a long straight stitch (secured with short couching stitches) and two straight stitches at bottom to form a V as shown on chart 1. Cut four 2¾in [7cm] lengths of yarn C and thread these under nose to form whiskers. Using yarn C, embroider French knots for eyes.

Sew together body pieces using backstitch, or mattress stitch if preferred, leaving a small opening. Insert toy filling and sew opening closed. Sew leg seams, leaving cast-on (upper) edge open. Insert toy filling, then sew upper edge closed. Attach upper edges to base of body. Sew arm seams, leaving cast-on (upper) edge open. Insert a little toy filling, then sew upper edge closed. Attach upper edges to body just below head shaping. Sew inner ears to outer ears, leaving cast-on edges open. Insert a little toy filling, then sew ears to head following chart 1.

BELLA BUNNY'S OUTFIT

Bella Bunny loves this skirt and top as they are good for dancing in.
She especially likes the silk ribbon—pale pink is her favorite color.

YARN
To fit bunny toy

Rowan RYC Cashsoft Baby DK and Cashsoft DK
A Baby DK Pale blue (805)   1 x 50g/1¾oz
B DK Gray (518)   1 x 50g/1¾oz
Note: For the alternative colorway, use DK
Pale mauve (501) for A and DK Brown (517)
for B.

NEEDLES & HOOK
1 pair of size 5 (3.75mm) needles.
Size E/4 (3.50mm) crochet hook.

EXTRAS
19½in [50cm] of narrow ribbon.

GAUGE
22 sts and 40 rows = 4in [10cm] square
measured over garter stitch using size 5
(3.75mm) needles.

SKIRT

MAIN PIECE
Using size 5 (3.75mm) needles and yarn A, cast
on 21 sts.
Row 1 (RS) Knit.
Row 2 Knit.
Row 3 K18 and turn.
Row 4 and every foll alt row Knit.
Row 5 K3 and turn.
Row 7 K6 and turn.
Row 9 K9 and turn.
Row 11 K12 and turn.
Row 13 K15 and turn.
Row 14 Knit.
Rep rows 1 to 14 twenty-seven times more.
Bind off.

FINISHING
Do *not* press.

Sew together cast-on and bound-off edges to
form center back seam using backstitch, or
mattress stitch if preferred.

Crochet edging
With RS facing, using size E/4 (3.50mm) crochet
hook and yarn B, attach yarn at base of back
seam and work around lower (longer) edge as
follows: *1sc into edge, ch1, rep from * to end,
join with a slip st to first sc. Fasten off.

Thread a length of yarn through waistline
(shorter) edge. Put skirt on bunny and pull yarn
to gather waistband tight enough to hold skirt
up, but loose enough to take on and off; then tie
yarn in a knot, remove and sew in ends. Thread
ribbon through "eyelet" holes 3 sts down from top
edge of skirt, and tie in a bow at center front.

TOP

BACK AND FRONT (both alike)
Using size 5 (3.75mm) needles and yarn B, cast
on 24 sts.
Work in g st throughout as follows:
Work 6 rows, ending with RS facing for next row.
Row 7 (RS) K3, (sl 1, K1, psso, K6) twice, sl 1, K1,
psso, K3. 21 sts.
Work 6 rows.
Row 14 (WS) (K3, sl 1, K1, psso, K2, sl 1, K1,
psso) twice, K3. 17 sts.
Work 6 rows.
Row 21 (RS) K3, sl 1, K1, psso, K7, sl 1, K1, psso,
K3. 15 sts.
Work 2 rows, ending with **WS** facing for next row.

Shape armholes
Dec 1 st at each end of next 2 rows. 11 sts.

Work 4 rows more, ending with **WS** facing for next row.

Shape neck
Next row (WS) K5 and turn.
Work each side of neck separately.
Dec 1 st at neck edge of next and foll alt row. 3 sts.
Work 3 rows more, ending with RS facing for next row.
Bind off.
With **WS** facing, rejoin yarn to rem sts, bind off center st, K to end. 5 sts.
Complete to match first side, reversing shapings.

FINISHING
Do **not** press.

Sew side and shoulder seams using backstitch, or mattress stitch if preferred.

Using yarn A, work crochet edging around neck, armhole, and lower edges as for skirt edging.

STRIPY TANK TOP

This colorful, roomy tank top is perfect with pajamas. It is ideal for all shapes and sizes.

BEFORE YOU BEGIN

YARN

Sizes	2-3 yrs	3-4 yrs	4-5 yrs
To fit chest	22in	24in	26in
	56cm	61cm	66cm
Actual size	26¾in	29in	31in
	68cm	74cm	79cm
Back length	11½in	12¼in	13½in
	29cm	31cm	35cm

Rowan RYC Cashsoft DK and Cashsoft Baby DK			
A DK Gray (518)	2	2	3 x 50g/1¾oz
B DK Pale blue (503)	1	1	1 x 50g/1¾oz
C DK Lime green (509)	1	1	1 x 50g/1¾oz
D Baby DK Pale green (804)	1	1	1 x 50g/1¾oz

NEEDLES

1 pair each of size 3 (3.25mm) and size 6 (4mm) needles.

GAUGE

22 sts and 30 rows = 4in [10cm] square measured over main pattern using size 6 (4mm) needles.

GETTING STARTED

BACK

Using size 6 (4mm) needles and yarn A, cast on 75 (81: 87) sts.
Row 1 (RS) *K2, P1, rep from * to end.
Row 2 Rep row 1.
These 2 rows form fancy rib.
Work 6 rows more in fancy rib, ending with RS facing for next row.
Joining in colors as required and beg with a K row, cont in striped St st as follows:
Using yarn A, work 2 rows.
Using yarn C, work 2 rows.
Using yarn A, work 2 rows.
Using yarn D, work 2 rows.
Using yarn A, work 2 rows.

Using yarn B, work 2 rows.
These 12 rows form striped St st.
Cont in striped St st until back meas 6¼ (6½: 7¾) in [16 (17: 20) cm], ending with RS facing for next row.

Shape armholes

Keeping stripes correct, bind off 6 sts at beg of next 2 rows. 63 (69: 75) sts.
Dec 1 st at each end of next 3 rows, then on foll 1 (2: 3) alt rows, then on foll 4th row. 53 (57: 61) sts.
Work even until armhole meas about 5 (5½: 6) in [13 (14: 15) cm], ending after 2 rows using yarn A and with RS facing for next row.
Break off contrasts and cont using yarn A only.

Shape shoulders and back neck

Next row (RS) Bind off 5 (6: 6) sts, K until there are 10 (10: 11) sts on right needle and turn, leaving rem sts on a holder.
Work each side of neck separately.
Bind off 4 sts at beg of next row.
Bind off rem 6 (6: 7) sts.
With RS facing, rejoin yarn A to rem sts, bind off center 23 (25: 27) sts, K to end.
Next row (WS) Bind off 5 (6: 6) sts, P to end.
Complete to match first side, reversing shapings.

FRONT

Work as given for back until 20 rows less have been worked than on back to beg of shoulder shaping, ending after 2 rows using yarn A and with RS facing for next row.

Shape neck

Next row (RS) K21 (22: 23) and turn, leaving rem sts on a holder.
Work each side of neck separately.
Keeping stripes correct, bind off 3 sts at beg of next row. 18 (19: 20) sts.

Dec 1 st at neck edge on next 3 rows, then on foll 2 alt rows, then on every foll 4th row until 11 (12: 13) sts rem.

Work 3 rows, ending after 2 rows using yarn A and with RS facing for next row.

Break off contrasts and cont using yarn A only.

Shape shoulder

Bind off 5 (6: 6) sts at beg of next row.

Work 1 row.

Bind off rem 6 (6: 7) sts.

With RS facing, slip center 11 (13: 15) sts onto a holder, rejoin appropriate yarn to rem sts, K to end.

Complete to match first side, reversing shapings.

FINISHING

Press pieces carefully on WS, using a warm iron over a damp cloth.

Sew right shoulder seam using backstitch, or mattress stitch if preferred.

Neckband

With RS facing, using size 3 (3.25mm) needles and yarn A, pick up and knit 21 sts down left side of neck, K across 11 (13: 15) sts on front holder, pick up and knit 21 sts up right side of neck, then 31 (32: 36) sts from back. 84 (87: 93) sts.

Work in fancy rib as given for back for 4 rows, ending with WS facing for next row.

Bind off knitwise (on **WS**).

Sew left shoulder and neckband seam.

Armhole borders (both alike)

With RS facing, using size 3 (3.25mm) needles and yarn A, pick up and knit 78 (84: 90) sts evenly all around armhole edge.

Work in fancy rib as given for back for 4 rows, ending with WS facing for next row.

Bind off knitwise (on **WS**).

Sew side and armhole border seams.

MOON HOT WATER BOTTLE COVER

Boys and girls everywhere will want a fantastic, embroidered hot water bottle cover like this one to cuddle up to.

BEFORE YOU BEGIN

YARN

Size of cover   8½ x 15½ in [22 x 39cm]

Rowan RYC Cashsoft DK and Cashsoft Baby DK

A	DK Gray (518)	2 x 50g/1¾oz
B	DK Lime green (509)	1 x 50g/1¾oz
C	Baby DK Pale green (804)	1 x 50g/1¾oz
D	DK Orange (510)	1 x 50g/1¾oz

NEEDLES

1 pair each of size 3 (3.25mm) and size 6 (4mm) needles.

BUTTONS

3

GAUGE

22 sts and 30 rows = 4in [10cm] square measured over St st using size 6 (4mm) needles.

GETTING STARTED

LOWER BACK

Using size 6 (4mm) needles and yarn A, cast on 27 sts.

Beg with a K row, work in St st as follows:
Work 1 row.
Cast on 6 sts at beg of next 2 rows. 39 sts.
Inc 1 st at each end of next 4 rows, then on foll alt row, ending with **WS** facing for next row. 49 sts.**

Work 43 rows, ending with RS facing for next row.
Change to size 3 (3.25mm) needles..
Next row (RS) K1, *P1, K1, rep from * to end.
Next row P1, *K1, P1, rep from * to end.
These 2 rows form rib.
Work 4 rows more in rib, ending with RS facing for next row.
Next row (RS) Rib 9, (bind off 3 sts, rib until there are 11 sts on right needle after bind-off)

twice, bind off 3 sts, rib to end.
Next row Rib to end, casting on 3 sts over those bound off on previous row.
Work 6 rows more in rib, ending with RS facing for next row. Bind off in rib.

FRONT

Work as given for lower back to **.
Work 9 rows, ending with RS facing for next row.
Using the *intarsia* technique, work next 54 rows foll chart (see page 106), which is worked entirely in St st beg with chart row 11 (a K row) and end at chart row 64.
Break off contrasts and cont using yarn A only.
Work 2 rows.

Shape top

Dec 1 st at each end of next 4 rows. 41 sts.
Bind off 3 sts at beg of next 2 rows. 35 sts.
Dec 1 st at each end of next 3 rows, then on foll alt row. 27 sts.
Work 1 row, ending with RS facing for next row.
Change to size 3 (3.25mm) needles.
Work in rib as given for lower back for 8in [20cm], ending with RS facing for next row.
Change to size 6 (4mm) needles.
Beg with a K row, work in St st as follows:
Work 2 rows.
Inc 1 st at each end of next 4 rows, ending with RS facing for next row. 35 sts.
Cast on 3 sts at beg of next 2 rows. 41 sts.
Inc 1 st at each end of next 4 rows. 49 sts.
Work 8 rows, ending with RS facing for next row.
Change to size 3 (3.25mm) needles.
Work in rib as given for lower back for 14 rows, ending with RS facing for next row.
Bind off in rib.

FINISHING

Press pieces carefully on WS, using a warm iron over a damp cloth.

Embroidery

Using yarn D, make a 2in [5cm] long tassel and attach to top of hat section of motif as in photograph. Using chart as a guide and yarn C, embroider French knots over hat. Using chart as a guide and yarns C and D, embroider stars in sky. For each small star, work three straight stitches and secure at center with a cross-stitch. For large star, work four straight stitches radiating out from center of cross motif and secure at center with a cross-stitch. Using yarn C, work French knots at ends of these straight stitches.

Overlap last 14 rows of front over last 14 rows of back and sew tog along side edges. Fold in half across center of narrow ribbed section, matching cast-on edges and sew front to back along all edges. Sew on buttons.

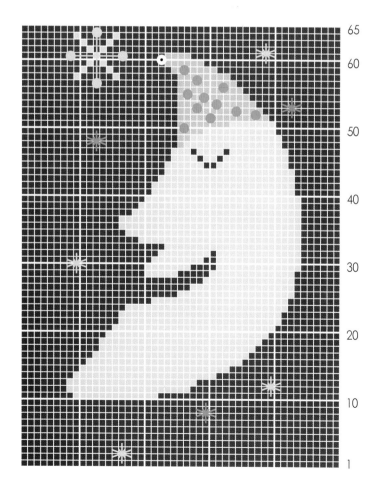

65
60
50
40
30
20
10
1

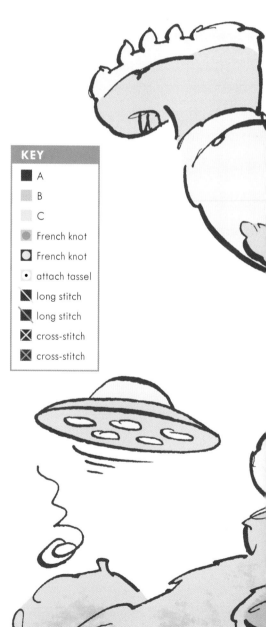

KEY	
■	A
■	B
□	C
●	French knot
◯	French knot
⊙	attach tassel
◤	long stitch
◣	long stitch
⊠	cross-stitch
⊠	cross-stitch

HOW-TO TIPS

FOLLOWING A KNITTING PATTERN

When working from the knitting patterns in this book, read the first section ("Before You Begin") carefully before you start knitting. This section gives you the size (or sizes) of the project, the amount of yarn needed, the recommended needle size, the knitting gauge, and any special abbreviations used (see page 110 for general abbreviations).

CHOOSING A SIZE

To choose the size of garment you want to knit, look at the age, the chest measurement the size fits, and the actual knitted measurement around the chest. The first figure given in multisized patterns is for the smallest size; the figures for the larger sizes follow in parentheses. If there is only one figure, it applies to all sizes. Be sure to follow the figures for your chosen size throughout.

CHECKING GAUGE

Obtaining the correct gauge will ensure a successful piece of knitting, so you should check your gauge before beginning. Using the recommended needles, knit a square in the pattern stitch and/or in stockinette stitch of about 5–10 more stitches and 5–10 more rows than those given in the gauge note. Press the finished square under a damp cloth and mark out the central 4in [10cm] square with pins. If you have too many stitches to 4in [10cm], try again using thicker needles. If you have too few stitches to 4in [10cm], try again using finer needles. Once you have achieved the correct number of rows and stitches to 4in [10cm], you will be able to knit the project to the correct measurements.

WORKING STRIPES

To avoid lots of loose ends when knitting stripes, drop the color you have finished using at the edge of the knitting; if it is needed later, just pick it up and start knitting with it again, but make sure you do not pull it too tightly up the edge.

Only break off colors if you need to start them at the opposite edge to where they have been dropped.

COLORWORK KNITTING

There are two main methods of working with more than one color in a single row of knitting—the intarsia and Fair Isle techniques. Intarsia produces a single thickness of fabric and is usually used where a color is only required in a particular area of a row and is not used across the whole row, as with the Fair Isle technique.

Intarsia

The easiest way to work the intarsia technique is to cut a short length of yarn for each motif or area of color. When changing colors, link one color to the next by twisting the yarns around each other on the wrong side to avoid holes in the knitting. Loose ends can either be darned-in later, or woven into the back during the knitting process. Weaving-in the ends while knitting is done in the same way as weaving-in yarns when working Fair Isle style knitting, and saves time darning-in ends later.

Fair Isle type knitting

When two colors are worked repeatedly across a row, strand the yarn not in use loosely across the wrong side of the knitting. If there are more than two colors, strand the floating yarns as if they were one yarn. Spread the stitches to their correct width to keep them elastic. For the best results, do not to carry the floating yarns over more than three stitches at a time, but weave them under and over the color you are working, catching them in on the wrong side of the knitting.

READING KNITTING CHARTS

Each square on a knitting chart represents a stitch and each line of squares represents a row of knitting. The key with the chart indicates what the colors and symbols on the chart mean; the colors on most of the charts in this book represent a specific yarn color, but on some charts they represent knit or purl stitches, so read the key carefully. The pattern instructions explain whether row 1 of the chart is a wrong-side or a right-side row. When working from the charts, be sure to read all right-side rows from right to left and all wrong-side rows from left to right.

Where a chart includes embroidery stitches, these are worked after the knitting has been completed and blocked.

PRESSING THE KNITTED PIECES

It is worthwhile finishing your knitting with care to achieve a truly professional look. Before blocking and pressing, darn in all yarn ends neatly along the selvage edge or a color join, as appropriate, using a blunt-ended yarn needle.

Block out each piece of knitting using pins, then gently press each piece on the wrong side, avoiding ribbing, garter stitch, or any other raised textured stitches and using a warm iron over a damp cloth. (Be sure to refer to the yarn label care instructions before pressing.) Take special care to press the edges, as this will make sewing seams both easier and neater.

SEWING PIECES TOGETHER

When sewing the knitted pieces together, remember to match areas of color and texture very carefully where they meet. Use a seam stitch such as backstitch or mattress stitch for all main knitting seams and sew all ribbing and neckbands with a flat seam, unless otherwise stated. Use slip stitch to sew pocket edgings and pocket linings in place.

For toys, most pieces can be sewn together with the right sides together and then turned right-side out. If the pieces are very tiny or narrow, however, they can be sewn together with the wrong sides facing. Use mattress stitch, backstitch, or overcast stitch for toy seams, as preferred.

After all the seams have been completed, press them carefully.

EMBROIDERY TECHNIQUES

Only a few simple hand stitches are used for the embroidery in this book. Always use a blunt-ended yarn needle (called a tapestry needle) when embroidering knitting and do not pull the yarn too tightly. Position the stitches as shown on the chart.

Couching

When the long straight stitches used are so long they might snag, secure them at intervals with short stitches.

French knot

To work a French knot, wrap the yarn several times around the needle and insert the needle back through the knitting near where it first emerged.

Cross-stitch

Work each cross-stitch with two slanting stitches as big as shown on the chart. All the top slanting stitches of the cross-stitches should face the same direction.

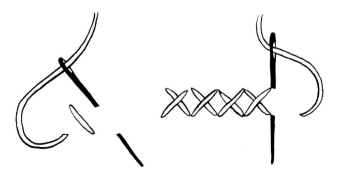

ABBREVIATIONS

KNITTING ABBREVIATIONS

The following are the standard abbreviations used in the knitting patterns in this book. Any special abbreviations used in a pattern are given with the instructions (for example, abbreviations for cables).

alt	alternate
beg	begin(ning)
cm	centimeter(s)
cont	continu(e)(ing)
dec	decreas(e)(ing)
foll	follow(s)(ing)
g	gram(s)
g st	garter stitch (K every row)
in	inch(es)
inc	increas(e)(ing); in row instructions work into front and back of stitch to make one extra stitch
K	knit
m	meter(s)
M1	make one stitch by picking up horizontal loop before next stitch and knitting into back of it
meas	measure(s)
mm	millimeter(s)
oz	ounce(s)
P	purl
patt	pattern(s) or work in pattern
psso	pass slipped st over
rem	remain(s)(ing)
rep	repeat(ing)
rev St st	reverse stockinette stitch (purl RS rows, knit WS rows)
RS	right side(s)
sl 1	slip one stitch onto right-hand needle
st(s)	stitch(es)
St st	stockinette stitch (knit RS rows, purl WS rows)
tbl	through back of loop
tog	together
WS	wrong side(s)
yd	yard(s)
yo	yarn over right needle to make a new loop
0 (zero)	no stitches, times or rows for that size

CROCHET ABBREVIATIONS

Crochet terminology is different in the US and the UK. The simple crochet instructions in this book are written in the US style. The list below gives the UK equivalent for the US terminology and abbreviations that appear in the knitting patterns on the previous pages.

US	UK
ch = chain	ch = chain
sc = single crochet	sc = double crochet
skip	miss
slip st = slip stitch	ss = slip stitch
sp(s) = space(s)	sp(s) = space(s)

YARN INFORMATION

The Rowan yarns used in this book are listed here. All the information was correct at the time of publication, but yarn companies change their products frequently and we cannot absolutely guarantee that the shades or yarn types used will be available when you come to use these patterns.

The yarn descriptions here will help you find a substitute if necessary. If substituting yarn, always remember to calculate the yarn amount needed by yardage rather than by ball weight.

Note: Although care instructions for yarns are given here, refer to the yarn label to confirm care recommendations, in case they have changed since the publication of this book.

ROWAN 4-PLY COTTON

Yarn type A lightweight cotton yarn.

Fiber content 100 percent cotton.

Ball size 50g/1¾oz; approximately 186yd [170m] per ball.

Recommended gauge 27–29 sts and 37–39 rows to 4in [10cm] measured over St st using sizes 2–3 (3–3¼mm) needles.

Care Machine washable on wool cycle in up to 104°F (40°C) water; do not bleach; dry flat, out of direct heat and sunlight (do not put in dryer); press with a warm iron only; dry-cleanable in all solvents.

ROWAN RYC CASHSOFT BABY DK

Yarn type A medium-weight wool-and-cashmere-mix yarn.

Fiber content 57 percent extra fine merino wool; 33 percent microfiber; 10 percent cashmere.

Ball size 50g/1¾oz; approximately 142yd (130m) per ball.

Recommended gauge 22 sts and 30 rows to 4in [10cm] measured over St st using size 6 (4mm) needles.

Care Machine washable on wool cycle in up to 86°F (30°C) water; do not bleach; dry flat, out

of direct heat and sunlight (do not put in dryer); press with a warm iron only; do not dry clean.

ROWAN RYC CASHSOFT DK

Yarn type A medium-weight wool-and-cashmere-mix yarn.

Fiber content 57 percent extra fine merino wool; 33 percent microfiber; 10 percent cashmere.

Ball size 50g/1¾oz; approximately 142yd (130m) per ball.

Recommended gauge 22 sts and 30 rows to 4in [10cm] measured over St st using size 6 (4mm) needles.

Care Machine washable on wool cycle in up to 86°F (30°C) water; do not bleach; dry flat, out of direct heat and sunlight (do not put in dryer); press with a warm iron only; do not dry clean.

YARN SUPPLIERS

For the best results, always use the yarn specified in your knitting pattern. Below is the list of distributors for Rowan handknitting yarns; contact them for where to buy Rowan yarn near you. For countries not listed, contact the main office in the UK or the Rowan website (www.knitrowan.com).

USA
Westminster Fibers Inc.,
4 Townsend West, Suite 8
Nashua, NH 03063.
Tel: (603) 886-5041/5043.
E-mail: rowan@westminsterfibers.com

AUSTRALIA
AUSTRALIAN COUNTRY SPINNERS, 314 Albert Street, Brunswick, Victoria 3056.
Tel: (03) 9380 3888.
E-mail: sales@auspinners.com.au

BELGIUM
PAVAN, Meerlaanstraat 73, B9860 Balegem (Oosterzele). Tel: (32) 9 221 8594.
E-mail: pavan@pandora.be

CANADA
DIAMOND YARN, 9697 St. Laurent, Montreal, Quebec H3L 2N1. Tel: (514) 388 6188.

DIAMOND YARN (TORONTO), 155 Martin Ross, Unit 3, Toronto, Ontario M3J 2L9.
Tel: (416) 736-6111. www.diamondyarn.com
E-mail: diamond@diamondyarn.com

DENMARK
Please contact Rowan Yarns for details of suppliers (see UK above).

FINLAND
COATS OPTI OY, Ketjutie 3, 04220 Kerava.
Tel: (358) 9 274 871. Fax: (358) 9 2748 7330.
E-mail: coatsopti.sales@coats.com

FRANCE
ELLE TRICOT, 8 Rue du Coq, 67000 Strasbourg.
Tel: (33) 3 88 23 03 13.
E-mail: elletricot@agat.net
www.elletricote.com

GERMANY
WOLLE & DESIGN, Wolfshovener Strasse 76, 52428 Julich-Stetternich. Tel: (49) 2461 54735.
E-mail: Info@wolleunddesign.de
www.wolleunddesign.de

COATS GMBH, Eduardstrasse 44, D-73084 Salach. Tel: (49) 7162/14-346.
www.coatsgmbh.de

HOLLAND
DE AFSTAP, Oude Leliestraat 12, 1015 AW Amsterdam. Tel: (31) 20 6231445.

HONG KONG
EAST UNITY CO. LTD., Unit B2,
7/F Block B, Kailey Industrial Centre,
12 Fung Yip Street, Chai Wan.
Tel: (852) 2869 7110. Fax (852) 2537 6952.
E-mail: eastuni@netvigator.com

ICELAND
STORKURINN, Laugavegi 59, 101 Reykjavik.
Tel: (354) 551 8258. Fax:(354) 562 8252.
E-mail: malin@mmedia.is

ITALY
D.L. SRL, Via Piave 24–26, 20016 Pero, Milan.
Tel: (39) 02 339 10 180.

JAPAN
PUPPY CO. LTD., T151-0051, 3-16-5 Sendagaya, Shibuyaku, Tokyo. Tel: (81) 3 3490 2827.
E-mail: info@rowan-jaeger.com

KOREA
COATS KOREA CO. LTD., 5F Kuckdong B/D, 935-40 Bangbae-Dong, Seocho-Gu, Seoul.
Tel:(82) 2 521 6262. Fax: (82) 2 521 5181.

NEW ZEALAND
Please contact Rowan Yarns for details of suppliers (see UK above).

NORWAY
COATS KNAPPEHUSET A/S, Postboks 63, 2801 Gjovik. Tel: (47) 61 18 34 00.
Fax: (47) 61 18 34 20.

SINGAPORE
GOLDEN DRAGON STORE, 101 Upper Cross Street #02-51, People's Park Centre,
Singapore. Tel: (65) 6 5358454.
E-mail: gdscraft@hotmail.com

SOUTH AFRICA
ARTHUR BALES PTY, P.O. Box 44644, Linden 2104.
Tel: (27) 11 888 2401.

SPAIN
OYAMBRE, Pau Claris 145, 80009 Barcelona.
Tel: (34) 670 011957.
E-mail: comercial@oyambreonline.com

SWEDEN
WINCENT, Norrtullsgatan 65, 113 45 Stockholm.
Tel: (46) 8 33 70 60.
E-mail: wincent@chello.se
www.wincentyarn.com

TAIWAN
LAITER WOOL KNITTING CO. LTD., 10-1 313 Lane, Sec 3, Chung Ching North Road, Taipei.
Tel: (886) 2 2596 0269.

Mon Cher Corporation, 9F No. 117 Chung Sun First Road, Kaoshiung. Tel: (886) 7 9711988.
Fax: (886) 7 9711666.

UK
Please contact Rowan Yarns for a complete list of UK suppliers:

ROWAN YARNS, Green Lane Mill,
Holmfirth, West Yorkshire HD9 2DX.
Tel: +44 (0) 1484 681881.
E-mail: mail@knitrowan.com
www.knitrowan.com

ACKNOWLEDGMENTS

Many thanks to all involved with this book and for all their hard work—especially to Susan whose idea it was and for her infinite patience, and to François whose illustrations and design are, as ever, marvelous.

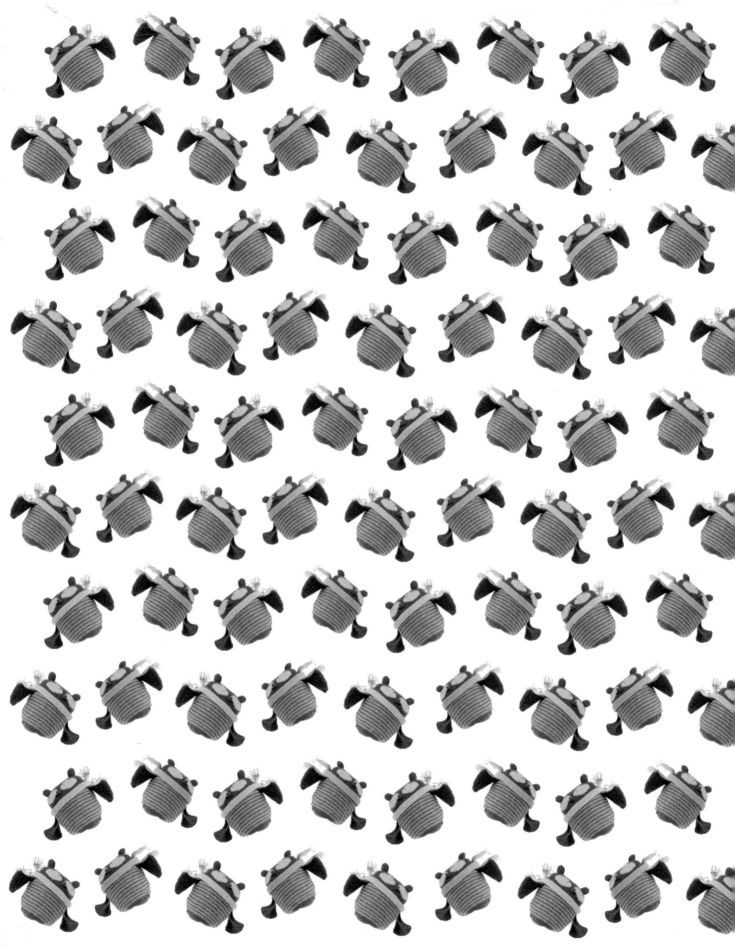